To: Mar

From: Ron Jarvis

Your wealth is
measured in hugs
not $.

FOXHOLE FATHER
THE FIELD GUIDE FOR FATHERS

BY

CHRISTOPHER R. WHALEN

Foxhole Father | Red Bank, NJ

Library of Congress Control Number: 2014916630

ISBN: 9780979352225

www.foxholefather.com

To Katelyn, Megan, and Jessica,
who gave me my life's mission: fatherhood.

To Mom and Dad, my first and best teachers.

FOXHOLE FATHER
THE FIELD GUIDE FOR FATHERS

"It is not the critic who counts; not the man who points out how the strong man stumbled, or where the doer of deeds could have done better. The credit belongs to the man who is actually in the arena; whose face is marred by dust and sweat and blood; who strives valiantly; who errs and comes short again and again. Who knows the great enthusiasms, the great devotions, and spends himself in a worthy cause. Who at the best knows in the end the triumph of high achievement; and who at the worst, if he fails, at least fails while daring greatly. So that his place shall never be with those cold and timid souls who know neither victory nor defeat."

– Theodore Roosevelt

TABLE OF CONTENTS

FOREWORD: LETTERS FROM MY CHILDREN

Although being a single parent is most often a difficult pursuit, my mother and father have both accomplished this feat successfully. My parents divorced when I was six years old, and events could have gone in a multitude of different ways. Fortunately for us three girls, our parents were able to maintain healthy relationships with all of us and raise us to be successful, independent women.

This book, written by my father, aims to help other fathers create loving relationships and environments for their children, even through difficult times. Throughout my entire childhood and young adulthood, my father has been unconditionally supportive and loving. Although his parenting has not been perfect, his everyday devotion to his daughters has been a constant reminder of what great parenting can be. His true dedication to being our Dad and always making us his first priority has definitely been a major part of my life, enabling me to become successful in any endeavor I pursue. I hope this book helps you or your significant other to make decisions during some of the tough times of being a parent.

- Katelyn Whalen

There is no such thing as a perfect parent. My father, the author of this book, is certainly no exception to that. Over the course of my life, he, like all parents, has made mistakes and errors in judgment when it comes to me and my sisters. Of course, this is not to discredit him, but rather to show you that parenting is difficult, particularly when you are a single parent.

After my parents' divorce, both my father and mother succeeded in raising three very different girls, sometimes together and sometimes apart. Despite the mistakes all parents are apt to make, I have never once doubted or been without the love, support, and protection of my parents. The core of their parenting is founded on putting their children above their own needs, and my father expounds on this idea at length in these pages.

Raising three girls alone for half of every week was not easy, but my father did it and did it well. My sisters and I are successful, well-rounded women, and that is the best reference I can give you for my father's parenting.

Again, no parent is perfect. But my father's mistakes have certainly taught him how to be a better person, man, and most importantly, a father. I have every confidence that this book will help you do the same.

- Megan Whalen

Growing up, it had always surprised me when I would hear that divorce was a bad thing. Before I entered elementary school, our parents had already decided to part ways, so having two homes was something I'd explain often to my friends but had no problem doing so. Mom and Dad had decided that it would be best for the week to be split into two sections so that we'd have just about the same time with both parents each week, and this, I feel, had the biggest impact on who my sisters and I are today.

Parents, just like all humans, are perfectly imperfect. There is no right or wrong way to be a parent, everyone's approach will vary and perhaps have additions. The addition to my dad's method of parenting was then having the challenge of being a single father raising three girls four days a week—a job not quite fit for everyone. The same cannot be said, however, for my dad; he just has a niche for being a dad. I don't necessarily mean being a dad by coddling us or staying out of our hormonal, crazy lives, but he guided us. Yes, there were the petty high school fights about grades, boys, and answering our cell phones, but as time went on, I grew to appreciate the undying care he had, because that's truly what most arguments are driven by. As I grew up, I did not by any means think either of my parents were perfect, but I could not think of a better pair.

With unconditional love, compassion, and patience (most of the time), my dad raised us to be independent, driven, and grounded. My dad held our hands until we let go, and when we did, he let us take our own path but always watched over us, letting us know he is always there.

- Jessica Whalen

OPEN LETTER TO THE MILITARY

I named this book Foxhole Father as the word "foxhole" truly describes my fathering mindset.

When I had my first child, I instantly felt that that my life had a higher calling and purpose. My sense of duty to my children found a kinship with the military life and the attributes that life embodied: service, fidelity, honor, selflessness.

I was so inspired by what it takes to be in the military that I patterned my fathering after it. And now, in this book, I am sharing my fathering success and have so many in the military to thank who have influenced me.

The feeling of living in a foxhole with my children brought me to learn of other military precepts and language. Those are the template for the hypervigilance and seriousness of my fathering mission.

I have never been in the military, but my family has gained so much from those who serve.

In honor of the men and women who have served our country, the military personnel I have known, and the authors of the field manuals, military theory books, and military essays I have read since becoming a father, this book serves as a testament of thanks to all of them.

You all have a part in my becoming the Foxhole Father.

In unending honor to those who have left our shores,

Christopher R. Whalen
Foxhole Father

MY STORY

Since 1997, I have been a single father to three daughters.

The year before, my children's mother and I decided it was best to divorce, and we agreed to share the physical and financial responsibilities between us. We agreed on equal parenting time. I would have all of the Fridays and Saturdays in our sharing arrangement. This would be a significant factor for me and my daughters when they entered their teen years

My daughters were six, five, and three years old at the time of the divorce.

My children's mother had been a stay-at-home mom, and I was out of the home every day trying to build my business to support us.

I voluntarily had taken the steps to divorce. In my heart, I knew these difficult steps were the best thing for all of us. Removing the children from the home and life they knew was a tough decision, but in the long run, the life they deserved lay elsewhere.

That "elsewhere" was not a fully formed vision in my mind, but my gut told me that staying married could hurt them emotionally in the long run.

I knew that getting divorced would allow me to become the father my daughters deserved. This would allow their mother and me to create separate homes that truly reflected our parenting styles.

Then suddenly, it became a reality. I was parenting these three precious lives on my own in our new home. I had planned to continue and expand upon my fathering philosophies that I'd used since my first child was born.

This book is the culmination of my day-to-day fathering experiences since 1990. My advice is direct, clear, and never sugar-coated. I always found the best parenting advice was given to me this way, so I have given it to you the same way here. This is not a flowery how-to book.

This book is a field manual for all fathers, regardless of their marital status or children's ages.

Why Foxhole Father? That is the only way I can find to describe how I felt when suddenly parenting my daughters on my own.

Dictionaries define a foxhole as:

(1)   A hole in the ground used by troops as a shelter against enemy fire or as a firing point

(2)   A place of refuge or concealment

(3)   A hole dug for a soldier to sit or lie in for protection from the enemy

My fathering mentality became exactly that. I had always been a fully participating parent when I was married, but I became truly hyperaware and hypervigilant about my fathering role the moment I became a single father.

It is clear that my daughters have benefited from this Foxhole Father mindset.

The night I officially moved us into our own apartment—March 16, 1997—was the night I became the Foxhole Father.

I was thirty-one years old and lying in a strange bed at 2:00 a.m. I had never lived alone. My three daughters, all under age seven, were quietly sleeping in their new bedroom for the first time.

I had spent the day with my daughters and my friends, moving us out of my marital home.

All day I maintained my happy facade, but now I lay in bed crying, hyperventilating and shaking uncontrollably. If I hadn't buried my face in a pillow, my uncontrollable sobbing would have woken my children.

What if they walked in my bedroom? What kind of emotional damage could have been inflicted on my daughters had they seen me like that? What if they saw the reality of the emotional wreck their father had become?

Three beautiful children in the next room, and I was completely responsible for them for the first time. I sat on the edge of my bed, unable to breathe. I had never had an anxiety attack at this level before. My tears were streaming down my face, and I was gasping for air. I tried to stand up, and the room started to spin. My eyes were open, but a deep blackness slowly filled my vision. I fell into the wall headfirst and was unconscious before I hit the floor. When I came to, I couldn't move.

I was on my back and still could not see. For three hours, my shaking, crying, and hyperventilating went on. I did my best to not wake my kids. There would be many more nights like this, alone, in the dark, trying to conceal my sorrow and fear from them, my mouth pressed hard into a pillow.

When the first rays of the sunrise entered my pitch-black room, a clear and deep vision came to me.

All of my fears were suddenly crystallized into one fathering mission: to put my children's needs and feelings first and to remove my needs and feelings from my parenting.

I had always thought I was putting their needs before mine, but my vision went much deeper than that.

This book shares that fathering vision with you.

My children are fully functioning adults now. They are flourishing in all areas of their lives.

I hope the fathering tools and philosophies I've shared in Foxhole Father will be of benefit to your family.

Christopher R. Whalen
Foxhole Father

YOUR FOXHOLE FATHER MISSION:

To raise your children to become fully functioning,
self-aware, self-respecting, self-sufficient,
and independent adults.

A Foxhole Father parents under these basic philosophies:

- To be the masculine, nonjudgmental sanctuary for his children
- To filter all thoughts and actions through the question, "What is best for my children?"

I have filtered every decision I have made since my first child was born through these simple ideas.

When you live the Foxhole Father mindset, all of your decisions for, and interactions with, your children become incredibly clear and simple.

All of your actions are seen as normal to your children, and they will eventually seek out those behaviors in relationships throughout their lives.

Because of this, your fathering actions, even the smallest ones, must be deliberate from now on.

You want your children to seek out your advice and help without any reservation or worry of judgment.

With the help of this book, you can learn how to become that masculine nonjudgmental sanctuary for your children.

You can teach them—simply by how you father them, live your broader life, and carry yourself in the world—what a father and a man are supposed to be.

No matter what your children's ages, you can become their Foxhole Father.

It is never too late.

This is your field guide to becoming a Foxhole Father.

Your mission starts now.

SECTION 1

QUICK ACTION GUIDE (QAG)

QUICK ACTION GUIDE (QAG)

Advice on 25 common fathering topics

Fathers, keep this with you! The objective of the Quick Action Guide is to provide general advice needed during urgent fathering situations. Sections 2 and 3 of this book provide expanded and detailed fathering direction.

TABLE OF CONTENTS

OAG 1 HOW TO TALK TO CHILDREN

1) Never use judgmental language such as:
* What is wrong with you?
* Do you think that is a good idea?
* You are a real disappointment.
* How could you be so stupid?
* You really screwed up again.
* You will never amount to anything.
* You are an embarrassment.

2) Tell/Ask your children the following things often:
* I love you.
* What can I do to make things easier for you?
* I know being a kid can be hard sometimes.
* I know you are a great person doing the best you can to navigate life.
* What do you think?
* How did that make you feel?
* I am always here to protect you, no matter what.
* I will never judge you.
* You can tell me anything.
* What thought process brought you to that conclusion?
* You never have to go through life's problems alone.
* I know, at your age, problems can seem overwhelming.
* I promise that together, we can make things OK.

See the chapter "Talking to Children – The Foxhole Father Philosophy," page 55, for more detailed direction.

QAG 2 SHOULD I EVER HIT MY CHILDREN?

No. Under no circumstances should you strike your child. This includes any punishment in which physical force is used and intended to cause some degree of pain or discomfort, however light, such as: hitting, spanking, slapping, caning, flogging, paddling, strapping and the use of a switch or rod.

Physically restraining children from doing something dangerous (i.e., stopping a three-year-old from running in the street) is expected.

Holding a child firmly in a time-out is sometimes necessary.

Raising a hand and hitting a child is never acceptable. Although it may certainly modify a child's behavior, the lessons it instills are regressive.

Avoid teaching your children that someone can say "I love you" in one moment and then physically assault them in the next. Teach them that this combination is unacceptable.

In the long run, hitting children teaches them the following regressive life lessons:

- Being assaulted by a loved one is acceptable.
- Controlling those you love by physical force is acceptable.

No matter how many times I read those two lines, I can never see them giving a child positive life outcomes.

A Foxhole Father never hits his children.

See the chapter "Should I Ever Hit My Children?", page 68, for more detailed direction.

OAG 3 CHILDREN AND TECHNOLOGY

Your children have a cell phone for YOUR convenience. You need to be able to call and text them. A cellular phone is a parenting tool to help run your household.

Your minor children do NOT need WEB-ENABLED smart phones. If you allow them to have one, you are putting them at extreme risk. Web-enabled means that they have full Internet access in their pockets at all times. This increases the risks of strangers contacting them through social networks, and it also means your children can access adult content. Remember, what you can see on your computer, they will be able to see on their phones: the entire World Wide Web. I would be very hesitant to allow teenaged and younger children to have web-based social networking applications on their phones.

You do not need web access to make calls or send/receive text messages or take pictures.

Wireless companies and home Internet service providers have excellent parental control options to limit the functionality your child has access to. Learn about them and use them today.

Home Networking and Computer Safety

At home, most of us have wireless networks with many devices connected to the Internet. Cable, optical and satellite companies all have parental control options that you can access for free simply by calling technical support.

The wireless router in your home is the first line of defense to control what content flows into your house. Learn how to password protect your routers and also how to block domains and words that you do not want your children to have access to at home.

Simply find the make and model of your router and go online and search for instructions on how to do these things. Don't be overwhelmed if you feel you are not tech savvy. Be patient with yourself, and have confidence that you can figure this out.

See chapter "Children and Technology", page 135, for further direction.

OAG 4 PLAYDATES
(SCREENING NEW FRIENDS/PARENTS)

There are some specific rules I recommend with regard to playdates. Many fathers are not comfortable demanding face-to-face meetings with other parents prior to allowing their children to socialize. I urge you to get over that shyness immediately. My suggestions:

1. Screen the parents.
Prior to allowing your children into someone else's home, I strongly urge you to physically meet both parents and screen them.

I wanted my children to interact with parents with similar parenting values. Meeting the parents of prospective playdates—both the mother and the father—and engaging them in deliberate discussions is the first part of the screening process. Your children are your greatest treasure; only entrust them to people you have fully screened. And only allow your children to socialize with children who have been raised with similar values, limits, and boundaries as yours.

Suggested questions:

- What types of pets do you have?
- How old are your other children?
- Do you have a pool?
- Is your backyard fenced in?
- Do you have any guns in your home?

2. Request to stay during the playdate.
Always request that you be allowed to stay at the house as well, especially during the initial playdate out of your home.

If you receive any negative reaction or an outright denial of your request to also attend, politely decline for you and your children. If you will be hosting a playdate, always request that a parent also attend, at least for the first one. Finding parenting compatibility is very similar to dating, and finding a "parenting" match can be just as elusive as finding a romantic partner. Following my rules will allow you to control the children and parents your children interact with. I cannot stress enough the importance of this on your children's development.

3. Set specific playdate start and finish times.

Very specific playdate time frames should always be agreed to.

Some parents may see you as a babysitter. I make sure to stress the importance of start and stop times for the playdates and state that I am expecting the other parents to arrive slightly before our agreed to playdate end time. Setting clear boundaries within your space is always best. If parents ignore your request for promptness, then their child may lose the benefits of being friends with yours.

4. Discuss the playdate with your children afterward.

If you are at a point where your child is going to other homes for playdates, you need to lightly discuss the experience with your child so you can gauge if the friend's home environment is a suitable place for your child. If you find that it is not suitable, then you will have to make the difficult but necessary fathering decision to disallow further playdates there.

Foxhole Fathering is NOT a popularity contest, and many of your decisions may be met with friction from your children. Your fathering conscience must guide you, and you must always filter your decisions based on what is best for your children, as opposed to what will make them the happiest.

Although my advice in this QAG may seem anti-playdate, the opposite is true. When I found parenting compatibility, playdates were an enriching part of my children's development.

You can apply these same screening guidelines throughout the teen years, but there is one slight change: Do not request attendance at the first "playdate" for your fifteen-year-old. I will save you the trouble. That will not go over well.

OAG 5 BEDTIMES/CURFEWS

Bedtimes
Keeping your kids on a schedule is extremely important. Maintaining schedules, limits, and boundaries is very important for their development. Children need a strong structure in order to develop properly and to feel safe and secure at all levels of their development. To be alert during the school day, adequate sleep is imperative.

1. Growing children need a lot of sleep.
2. Strict bedtimes should be enforced, especially on school nights.
3. Computers and phones should be turned off at bedtime.
4. Children should never have televisions in their rooms.

Curfews
The same logic applies to curfews.

QAG 6 DO YOU FEEL GUILTY ABOUT SOMETHING?

One day, when one of my daughters was seven or so, I failed to get to the bus stop after school on time and she was brought back to school. I was called and simply picked her up there.

To this day I still feel guilty, as if I had failed and abandoned her. She is an adult now and doesn't recall it even happening. In fact, she consoles me over it!

You are going to make mistakes. You are human. You are going to do things and then instantly regret them. It happens to me even to this day.

You know who never feels guilty or regretful? Heartless and selfish people who have only their own needs on their minds.

If you are doing your best for your children, then you should never feel guilty when you fall short and sometimes fail.

Guilt is like anger; it serves no positive purpose for you or your children.

You will lose patience, raise your voice, and sometimes forget something important to your children. You may just be too tired to keep a promise to them.

Learn from your mistakes, discuss those mistakes with your children openly and with sincerity, and ask for forgiveness when necessary.

Then let it go, free yourself from guilt, and take it as a teaching moment for YOU and just try your best again tomorrow.

OAG 7 NAMING YOUR CHILDREN

When naming your children, make sure you give them names that are very easy to understand and that are easily pronounced by strangers so your child does not have to continually tell people how to pronounce his or her name.

A good example is Teresa instead of Theresa.

I once knew someone whose name was Teresa. The second e was soft, which means it was pronounced like the e in the word egg.

Everyone who read her name pronounced it like the name Theresa, where the second e was pronounced like the first e sound in the name Eve.

I am sure she is still correcting the pronunciation of her name often.

My point is that what you name someone will impact them until they die. You should be very careful when you do it.

Make sure that everyone will be able to easily read the name correctly and know exactly what the name is. Parents often take it as some kind of artistic or creative job to give their kids interesting names. In these instances, the child's need is ignored. A child's name should not be a lifelong talking point or a way for parents to make a statement.

If I had decided to leave the U.S. and live full time in another country, you can be sure I would have researched that culture's first names and tried to find one using the same instructions I gave above.

Christopher might make perfect sense in America, but in Nepal, for example, my child named Christopher would have been in the Teresa-Theresa quandary. That is never good. The top five male Nepalese names are:

1. Raju
2. Ram

FOXHOLE FATHER - QUICK ACTION GUIDE   1 3

3. Hari
4. Jitendra
5. Rajendra

There would have been a Raju or Ram Whalen hiking up Mount Kusum Kangguru had I had a child in Nepal.

And by the way, I just learned that Teresa legally changed her name to Jill.

OAG 8 LYING

The fact that your child lied to you is bad for them, not you.

It is normal for your children to keep the truth from you sometimes and even to flat out lie to you. There are varying degrees of lying, and it is important that you try to understand the emotions and intentions within your children for keeping a truth from you.

I understand that there is not always time to be patient. Your child may be at physical risk or in some other form of jeopardy, and you will need to do all you can to find out the truth so they can avoid harm. There will be time for calm talk later, after the danger has passed.

But in situations where there is no imminent risk, I have found a successful approach to dealing with a child's lies that may have the best possible outcomes for everyone.

Many parents get agitated and even enraged when they realize their children have lied deliberately. They may be interpreting the lie as a personal attack. This is something you need to avoid.

A Foxhole Father considers what he may have done to precipitate his child not being comfortable telling him the truth.

Observe your emotions during these times and work to control them. Once you have controlled your emotional reaction and personal feelings, you can then deliberately father your children based on their needs.

You need to start with a loving and respectful discussion that focuses on the reasons for the lying. The reason your child lied is much more important than what he lied about.

- Why wasn't he comfortable telling you the truth?
- What can you do to make him more comfortable in the future?
- Does he know that you will never judge him?

Most times the specific thing that is causing friction, in this case a lie, will soon be forgotten. So, along that line, you need to have a broader discussion about your relationship with your child and try to understand why this lie has happened.

Some options are:

- Your child simply wants privacy with regard to the topic.
- Something has happened to cause your child to not feel comfortable talking to you.
- Your child is not comfortable with the topic and may be embarrassed.
- Someone may have demanded that your child not discuss it with you.
- Your child may fear your disapproval or interference.

Take this opportunity to build even greater trust within your child so that he or she feels more comfortable being honest with you in the future.

Remember, this is not about you, and injecting your personal hurt or fear into the discussion may ruin the teaching moment that you have in front of you.

You want to avoid that from happening at all costs.

Take the opportunity to do rare parenting here. You should not show anger. You should not raise your voice.

Your children do not have to consider your personal feelings. Injecting your personal feelings will only delay a positive outcome for your child.

The fact that your child lied to you is bad for them, not you.

(F) Children need to understand why we dont lie, also.

OAG 9 DISOBEDIENCE IN PUBLIC

My long-term parenting goal was to create functioning adults. That started with teaching them acceptable behaviors. When children don't act properly, many times frustration, anger, and impatience guide the parenting.

Once a child can understand basic conversation, you need to discuss why they need to obey you or to stop acting in a certain way.

Avoiding the stereotypical escalation that disobedience often brings out is a good start.

The following is a good example of ineffective parenting that teaches poor lessons.

Ten-year-old Timmy and his family are at a barbeque. Dad is sitting in the shade drinking a beer. Timmy has turned on the hose and is spraying random people on the other side of the yard.

Dad does not move but simply yells at Timmy over and over again, each time getting louder. We have all seen this countless times.

"Timmy, stop doing that ..."

"Timmy, stop doing that ..."

"Timmy, stop doing that ..."

"TIMMY, STOP DOING THAT!"

My suggestions:

- Do not parent from a distance as described above.
- Never reprimand your child loudly and openly in front of others.
- Go and speak directly and calmly with your child and explain why the behavior is inappropriate.
- You may need to physically stop your child. This never means

striking, but it may mean restraining.
* Remember, expressing anger can only be destructive.
* Remember, this is a teaching moment for your child.

You want your children to be curious. That is the basis of learning. Children will do many things that we don't like because of that curiosity. A garden hose with water shooting out of it would make any child curious.

The Foxhole Father should have confidence that he can teach his children acceptable behaviors and valuable life lessons without angry, loud, and violent reactions.

Sometimes, when children are very young, they are exposed to frightening reactions from their parents, and this can only instill evasiveness in them. We want to build a trusting, open, and accepting atmosphere, even when we are teaching them rules, limits, and boundaries they need to adhere to.

Remember, the goal is teaching life skills and behaviors that will make them successful. So, in all instances, you need to show them which behaviors they should not be engaging in and, most importantly, why.

I disagree, cleaning your room is a simple discepline, that sets the tone for everything else,

OAG 10 CLEAN YOUR ROOM!

Does it really matter if your child's room is perfectly clean?

Just like our desks at work, or our cars, people keep their bedrooms in different states of neatness and organization. Just because a child's room has a lot of clutter does not mean the room is "dirty."

A disorganized room is not an indication of immaturity or an emotional problem. Many of us can function in what looks like total chaos to an outsider.

If you find that the organization in your children's room is causing functional problems in their lives, then definitely guide them to make changes to fix those problems.

My advice is to relax the broad "clean your room" rule and replace it with specific rules:

The following worked well for me:

- All food and plates must be removed from the bedroom prior to your children going to bed.
- Your children's clothes must be regularly washed.
- Your children's clothes should be stored in their rooms in such a way to assure your children look presentable when wearing the clothes in public.

All children, like adults, are very different when it comes to organizing their spaces. Give them the respect they deserve, and allow them to maintain their space in a clean way—yet their way.

One of your children may neatly fold clean clothes in drawers and hang them on hangers. Another of your children may live out of a laundry basket during the week. Either way, you want to teach them the benefit of going out into public in clean and unwrinkled clothes.

Since becoming a father in 1990, I have never told my children to clean their rooms. As long as your child can function and do the things for which they are responsible, then their room organization does not matter.

Again, everyone is an individual. Just like other personal preferences, the level of organization that someone maintains in his or her bedroom is also very unique and may be very different from yours.

So, if you examine this issue through one of my basic Foxhole Fathering tenets, you will ask yourself, "Is this really bad for my child?" If, objectively, you cannot see any true negative impact on your child for having a disorganized room, then I would not mention it.

Disorganized does not mean dirty. Try reducing your demands on your child to clean his or her room down to my three basic rules above.

Most importantly, this can reduce household friction on a topic that so many families quarrel about unnecessarily.

I would discuss this entire QAG section with your children. It may teach them to have a new attitude and objective thought process toward this and other topics.

+ make bed
+ organize all tiddy n before
bed each night.

OAG 11 CHILDREN'S SEXUAL BEHAVIOR

Many parents build an atmosphere of fear around sex. This happens well before a child matures enough to have a sexual urge.

This is a big mistake.

The Foxhole Father never demonizes any behavior that will eventually be considered normal, including sex. Sex is the most normal behavior, and today, more than ever, our children are bombarded with sexual imagery, words, and thoughts.

Did you discover your child engaging in sexual behavior, or learn that he or she is homosexual or transgender?

You will have strong emotions about these things. But you don't have to let them guide your parenting. Avoid having an emotional (selfish) reaction.

Remember, you are the main educator of your children, and this situation is one of the most personal for them. Your reactions will be forever imprinted in their hearts and minds. It can be a great teaching moment if you allow it to be.

Important Note: You have very little control over your children's sexual behavior, and no control over their sexual orientation. If you believe that you do, please reread the last sentence until you don't.

You must be realistic. Unless you are physically with them twenty-four hours a day, they will behave in ways you believe are bad for them.

You have to make a decision:

1.   Are you going to educate them in a nonjudgmental way about sex?

OR

2.   Are you going to attempt to dictate how they will sexually behave from now on?

Number 2 was not possible, so I chose number 1 with my daughters. That is my advice to you.

So, your child has engaged in sexual behavior, or shared with you that he or she is homosexual or transgender. One emotion you may feel is anger. Anger is always destructive, and it has no place in your parenting at any time.

You have a great opportunity to build a stronger bond with your child if you act deliberately and thoughtfully.

The Foxhole Father makes this solely about his child. Use this as the teaching moment that it is.

If you have had healthy communication with your children from birth, you have a greater chance that your child was responsible and used birth control. This communication should have included frank discussions about the dangers of sex: pregnancies, STDs, and how to prevent them. Your child may have even discussed his choice to become sexually intimate before it happened with you.

How old is your child? Is he old enough and mature enough to be engaging in sexual behavior? You will have to determine your child's current stage of development before going forward with your parenting.

You must be realistic, though. Depending on their age and mobility outside of your home, it will not be possible to stop your children from engaging in sexual activity.

Now that you know your child is sexually active, you need to discuss being responsible about it.

- Strongly suggest that girls begin using birth control, both your daughters and your sons' partners.
- Make sure all of your sexually active children have access to condoms and that those condoms are used ALWAYS, even if the females are already using some other form of birth control.
- Educate your children about STDs. Reinforce to them that they should require all potential sexual partners be tested for STDs before any physical contact, even kissing.

Herpes is for life, and you can contract genital herpes in your mouth through oral sex. That means you can become orally infected with genital herpes by kissing someone who already is.

This website has excellent information on Herpes: http://www.nlm.nih.gov/medlineplus/ency/article/000857.htm

AIDS is incurable and often fatal. HPV is the most common sexually transmitted infection and it can cause health problems like genital warts and cancer.

Discuss how sex should be accompanied by an adult-level romantic love and a true commitment to monogamy. These two things are hard, if not impossible, to find as a teenager. You must have a clear discussion about where your child is emotionally and how teenagers quite often fool themselves into believing they are in an "adult" love.

If you have established respectful and open communication with your child, which includes making their needs and safety the basis for that communication, then discussions about sex can simply carry on that tradition, and your children will be open to discussing how sex can impact them and how to protect themselves from the potential harm that can accompany it.

Teach them responsible sexual behavior, explaining all the while why it is best for them. Those lessons should start well before they are in an intimate relationship.

QAG 12 PEER PRESSURE

Most situations in which your children are being influenced by peer pressure are temporary.

Focus on the emotions that are acting on your child and explain what a trap these are.

During some developmental stages, children may have an intense and anxious desire to fit in at all costs. During these times their self-esteem and confidence may be suffering. Most of us have fallen for the power of peer pressure as children, and, unfortunately, many adults carry this into adulthood and are constantly worried about whether they will be accepted by various peer groups.

Some children are genetically predisposed to shyness and insecurity, but many children learn social insecurity by watching the actions of their parents. Children take their social cues from their parents. Parents constantly seeking approval and validation from others will have children who do the same.

Parents may unknowingly exert pressure for their children to dress and act mainstream, and this can suppress their children's individual style. It can be just as bad for a child's development as falling for peer pressure.

Take a personal inventory and evaluate how you are projecting yourself as a man to the world. Are you trying to maintain a look, obtain more objects, or engage in certain behaviors out of fear of being rejected by a peer group? If you are, you may be silently teaching a harmful life lesson to your children.

When your children are falling victim to these behaviors and fears, this is the time to have a much broader discussion about how peer pressure works, why it is something to be ignored, and why your child's individuality and personal desires must be considered first, before the demands of any group or person.

If your child's personal desires match those of the crowd, that is a great start. If not, guide your child down the path of confidence and individuality.

These situations are some of the most significant teaching moments you will have.

Teaching a child how to fight peer pressure and to learn decreased importance of group acceptance will be traits that will help them the rest of their lives.

See the chapter "Desperation Leads to Self-Compromise Leads to Enslavement," page 90, for more detailed discussion on this topic.

QAG 13 SCHOOL ADMINISTRATOR /TEACHER ISSUES

You are the main educator of your child. I want you to say this out loud.

"I am the main educator of my child."

Quite often you will need to remind school employees of this fact. School employees, especially teachers, are both a resource and an influence on your child. They need to be monitored just as much as your children do.

Quite often school administrators and teachers believe they are running an autonomous and enclosed world and that they are above the scrutiny of anyone outside of what they consider their domain.

Let each teacher know at the start of each year that you, your child, and that teacher are all working together for the betterment of your child; however, you are the main educator of your child.

Politely convey that you will expect that teacher to communicate any issues with you directly and that the teacher has a responsibility to make sure that your child attains the highest grade possible in his or her class. Get each teacher's email and contact information.

Waiting for midterm progress reports is much too late to correct problems your child may be experiencing. This must be done almost daily.

Many schools have an online system for tracking grades, attendance, and teachers' notes. You should check this regularly to monitor your child's progress but also to make sure that the teachers are updating information every day. I have found countless errors in grading over the years that could have brought my children's grades down. Updating of your child's performance records on a daily basis is one of a teacher's most important functions to support you in parenting your child properly.

Too often, the monitoring of grades can lead to friction with your children. Properly communicating to your children that you are their ally and only want to help them achieve their very best is crucial.

See my chapter "School/Activities – You Are the Main Educator of Your Children," page 115 for more detailed advice.

QAG 14 DAUGHTER'S FIRST PERIOD/ SON'S NOCTURNAL EMISSIONS

Many fathers are embarrassed to talk about the female body and topics like menstruation. You need to educate yourself on these subjects, and then educating your child becomes much easier.

Some girls can begin menstruating as young as ten. Some boys experience nocturnal emissions as early as thirteen. Well before your children experience these things, make sure they have been informed and well prepared ahead of time. Yes, there may be too young an age to start to talk about these topics. You will have to gauge when the moment is right. Your sons and daughters should be taught about bodily functions and why they happen, how they happen, and how to take care of themselves when they occur.

Your son may experience nocturnal emissions (wet dreams) at a much younger age than you probably expect. As you probably experienced these yourself, you should be in a confident position to prepare him.

The Foxhole Father is not embarrassed to discuss anything with his children.

It does not matter what the topic is. From the moment you begin communicating with them, remember that you're striving to be their nonjudgmental will be able to easily read the name correctly and know... masculine safe place. That means guiding them and helping them through every part of their lives, including things that make them female or male.

The more comfortable you are, the more comfortable they will be with you, themselves, and their body. The lesson here is that discussions about such things need to start well before these events actually happen to them. If you have built the right foundation of nonjudgmental communication, then these types of discussions will be easy for you and your children.

Avoiding such topics as these can often lead to children feeling embarrassed about their bodies. Relegating these types of discussions to their mother is very common, but this is completely unnecessary and can create a disconnect between you and them.

The Foxhole Father establishes the standards by which his children will judge other people, especially men.

Always be mindful that your behavior is what they will view as normal and acceptable. You need to project the type of person you want your children to emulate and to develop relationships with.

Remember, you are building a foundation of communication that will always go well beyond the topic at hand. You're trying to establish open communication with your children from the first moments you speak to them. This can last a lifetime.

The Foxhole Father strategy you need to take from this section is this: From the moment your children are born and you begin communicating with them, communicate openly, calmly, and without reservation, no matter the subject matter.

For your sake and for all of your children's sake, both sons and daughters, if you are embarrassed or hesitant to speak about any topic, work as hard as you can to get past that and to change yourself. Do not stop until you can speak directly and without reservation at all times.

You can definitely achieve this. When you do, your entire family will flourish, and you all will grow ever closer.

This website has some guidance on discussing menstruation:
http://kidshealth.org/parent/positive/talk/talk_about_menstruation.html

This website has some guidance on understanding boys and puberty:
http://kidshealth.org/kid/grow/boy/boys_puberty.html

QAG 15 KIDS AND ALCOHOL/DRUGS/TOBACCO USE

The discovery of a child using alcohol, drugs, or tobacco can be one of the most frightening events for a parent. You need to keep your emotions in check. This moment of discovery on your part should be a teaching moment and one in which your child feels respected and not judged. If your initial reaction is to yell, verbally abuse, or chastise your child, take a moment to pause and revisit that discussion at a later time when you can focus your energy on your child.

Remember, all the signs from society say that using alcohol, drugs, and tobacco are normal behavior. We may believe that these are "adult" behaviors and off limits for children. But these behaviors are seen as mature and normal to children, as that is how they are projected by society.

And what teenager ever believed he or she was still a child? None!

With that said, underage drinking and tobacco use and taking drugs are illegal activities that can lead to a permanent criminal record. Do all that you can to restrict your children's activities outside of your home if they are taking those opportunities to do any of these things.

The combination of the potential of great physical harm and getting arrested makes this a subject to be taken extremely seriously, and your parenting needs to rise to the level it deserves.

Alcohol is a drug. To me, the only true difference between alcohol and drugs is alcohol's legality.

If you go beyond a social drink, show any physical signs of alcohol affecting you, use tobacco, or do drugs, you are teaching your children that taking a mind-and-body-altering substance is acceptable and condoned by you. Combine parental use with the constant exposure and access to alcohol, drugs, and tobacco that children have, and it should not surprise any parent when his child is also using them.

Do you drink to the point where alcohol affects you? Do you smoke? Do you do drugs? Then how can you attempt to disallow your children from doing the same? Can you tell them they are not allowed? Of course you can. Will it make you look like a hypocrite and foolish? Of course it will.

You are to blame if your children are copying your destructive behaviors, and you should apologize for setting a bad example.

The Foxhole Father is never impaired in front of his children, even the slightest amount.

The discussions about alcohol, drugs, and tobacco should start long before your children have access to them and should focus on responsible and safe behaviors.

When you see someone even slightly impaired in front of your children, use it as a teaching moment. I always did.

It is unrealistic to assume your children will never drink alcohol or take a drug. As they get older, your ability to keep them from doing things greatly diminishes.

You need to teach them all of the dangers involved in all of these activities.

Tell your sons and daughters that if they feel the need to change their mental state with drugs or alcohol to speak to you about this immediately. Some people have chemical imbalances and attempt to self-medicate. Make sure your children understand this concept in case they experience this themselves someday. Discuss family history and how genetics can play a major role in addiction.

Keep prescription medications under lock and key in your home, especially those known to lead to addiction, like pain pills.

Prescription painkilling drugs like Demerol, Vicodin, Codeine and OxyContin are extremely addictive. Teens who are prescribed painkilling medications are at extreme risk for addiction. Do all you can to avoid these being prescribed for your child by a doctor. According to a presentation at the American Society of Addiction Medicine 42nd Annual Medical Scientific Conference, sixty-seven percent of teens who were admitted for painkiller addiction were given prescriptions for those drugs in the previous year.

Teach your children about the importance of designated drivers. Let them know that if they, or the driver they are out with, are unable to drive safely that you will pick them up, no questions asked. Tell your daughters how often girls are sexually assaulted when they believe the boys they are drinking with are "safe." Educate your children about the epidemic of rape on college campuses.

This is also a great time to discuss peer pressure. See my chapter on peer pressure, "Desperation Leads to Self-Compromise Leads to Enslavement," page 90 for an explanation of how I believe peer pressure can be discussed with your children.

By example, you can teach your children as I have. My children have never seen me drink alcohol or take an illegal drug, so I have never been impaired in front of them. Children should never see their parents affected by alcohol or narcotics, ever. It can be incredibly frightening for children to see their parents "buzzed" and acting and talking strangely.

My children have learned through my actions that they can be functioning and happy people without mind-altering substances (alcohol and drugs). This example has made them stronger and able to make safer decisions.

To restate, if you do drink alcohol, take drugs, or use tobacco, you are giving your children permission to do the same. They will believe it is an acceptable behavior, no matter what you say.

Don't be like some parents I have known. They drink often and to excess, while telling their children to never drink. The parent who does this confuses his children and is seen as a pure hypocrite.

Will this be difficult for some of you? Definitely.

The Foxhole Father always does the right thing, no matter how difficult.

QAG 16 CO-ED SLEEPOVERS

Should boys and girls have sleepovers at any age? Many parents dismiss this idea completely without thinking it through. Every situation needs to be assessed individually and discussed.

When your child asks you to have a sleepover with both boys and girls, please fight your initial reaction to say, "Are you out of your mind? Absolutely not, never, ever!"

Most parents immediately have images of underage children having sex in their living room at 3:00 a.m.

Our fears about sex can quickly become the focus of our thoughts in these situations. I would suggest you ignore those initial thoughts if you have them. They may make you overreact. Try to not allow your anxieties to become the focus of the conversation. Put the focus on your children.

Let's look at what is really happening. Your child is innocently asking for something, which could be very significant for their development, and you should address it calmly.

That was exactly how I handled the question from my twelve-year-old, even though my internal reaction was extreme! I wanted to scream, "Are you out of your mind? Absolutely not, never, ever!"

All of my children had male and female friends since they were young, and it simply made sense to them that they would invite both male and female friends to sleep over at our house.

My daughter said: "Dad, after the movies on Friday, me and my friends wanted to come back here and play the new video game you got me for Christmas. We all talked about it, and it would be fun if they could stay over."

After pausing and pushing down my extreme initial reaction, I was open with my daughter about it and said the following:

"This is one of those parenting moments I was not prepared for! My initial and immediate reaction was to say, 'Absolutely not!' without even thinking about it."

We discussed it openly, and I admitted my initial reaction was wrong in this case. I said I would agree to it. We laid out some ground rules, and then I spoke to the other parents involved. The other parents were happy to hear my calm plan, and the entire night was a great success.

There were only three pregnancies! Just kidding ...

My open discussion about my initial reaction and then working together with my child to develop a plan that met all of our needs was a great moment for both of us. There would be many more in the future.

The Foxhole Father is a collaborative father.

Also see my chapter "Boys and Girls Interacting," page 126.

QAG 17 CAR DATES/DRIVING WITH NON-FAMILY

Unless you know the non-family member well and know they have adequate driving experience, you should disallow your child from being a passenger in someone's car.

This applies to car dates and to driving with friends.

This rule is very similar to the rules I discuss regarding playdates.

Teenagers today, with the aid of social networking, have a much larger circle of friends than we did. In my mind, this is a greater circle of strangers that needs to be monitored. This means you need to be much more alert than fathers of thirty years ago.

Always make sure you meet all people your teenagers are spending time with and meet their parents, as well. Make no exceptions. This may cause friction, but fathering the right way can do that.

The Foxhole Father does not back down.

I made my home open and welcoming 24/7 for my kids' friends. This made them comfortable with bringing new friends home to hang out. My children spent more time in my home than in the homes of their friends.

If you have established good communication and empowered your children to consider their needs and safety first, then they will naturally tend toward being thoughtful about who they spend time with and who they get into cars with.

That is your goal here.

QAG 18 PETS - DADDY, WE WANT A PUPPY!

There is a strong urge in some parents to give into a child's request for a pet, especially a puppy. Feelings that a home is not complete without a puppy, as well as feelings of guilt if you don't get your child one, can really make you act hastily.

A pet, especially a puppy, requires an incredible investment in time, and no matter how enthusiastic your children are, the majority of the responsibility for pet care may fall on the shoulders of you and your partner.

Having a dog is no different than having another child to take care of. Dogs are much different than cats or goldfish. Parents have such limited time today, and it is OK for both of you to consider this.

Even if your children seem willing to help with a pet's care, they may lose interest after a short time. Also, don't get a pet for which your children cannot fully participate in its care. A dog, which requires walks outside, sometimes early in the morning, would only make sense when the children are old enough to handle such a responsibility safely on their own.

My advice is to start with a pet that does not require you to leave the house to maintain it. That will limit the physical responsibilities of its care.

If you are separated from your children's mother, I urge you to NOT take on the responsibility of any pet within the first twenty-four months of the separation unless you are sure it will not become a burden on you.

QAG 19 IS YOUR TEENAGER WORKING YET?

As children enter high school, their social lives increase, and so does the money needed to finance that life.

I see eighteen-year-old children who have never worked to support themselves. This is a great disservice to those children. Your children need to work in order to support their social lives. It is that simple. I am not talking about doing chores at home for an allowance. I never gave my children an allowance for household chores. They live in the house, so cleaning and maintaining it is something they must learn to do naturally and without pay.

Finding a paying job for a fourteen-year-old can be challenging.

Babysitting is always a great option. Yes, even for boys.

Look to friends and neighbors who made need assistance around their homes or local business owners who might have some hourly work.

Cutting grass, shoveling snow, raking leaves, and assisting with painting and other household work can be a steady stream of income from your neighbors for your daughters and sons.

Instilling a work ethic leads to your teen earning his or her own money, which leads to self-esteem and pride, which leads to a stronger work ethic, which leads to them earning more of their own money …

Earning their own money and budgeting that money for their own purchases and savings is great financial training for any young person. This life lesson needs to be taught as early as possible. It also gives your children an appreciation and understanding for what it takes for you to put money in your wallet.

Managing money they have earned from hard work is one of the most important life lessons you can teach your child.

QAG 20 KIDS' GRADES AND EXTRACURRICULAR ACTIVITIES

Now let's talk about your child's academic performance.

This can become a source of great friction with your child if it is not handled the right way.

Your children's grades can have a significant impact on their future, especially if they plan to attend college. This should be taught when they start receiving grades in school, but in a way in which you are both working together toward an important life goal.

Extracurricular activities are also important for development from the youngest ages. Their benefits should be taught as well. Many children find their life's path through them.

What if your children aren't performing at their best academically? Poor academic performance can hurt their future opportunities. You should do all you can to help them achieve their best grades.

Each child's academic best will be different.

Many parents today spend zero time reviewing homework and projects with their children. You need to be different.

My "grade" goals for my children were based on them as individuals. I monitored their grade levels each week. If they were not working up to their individual potential, this meant my child needed to spend more time studying and less time doing other activities. This may mean you stay in with your child on a weekend as well as weeknights until his or her grades are brought up to the correct levels.

This may mean time away from activities and friends your children love. Do not give into the pressure and emotional outbursts you may experience from them.

These are the moments where you have to be the parent and enforce rules and boundaries that are in your child's long-term best interest.

So many parents fail to do this, and this can prevent your children from achieving all they can in life.

Remember, you are the main educator of your children. Academic performance will impact all of their life's opportunities. You have to make sure, no matter the struggles you go through and the friction your children present to you, that they achieve the best grades they possibly can.

Many parents do not have the strength or foresight to enforce such demanding restrictions if a child's academic performance is suffering. Many parents will buckle under and not curtail other activities even if their child's grades are slipping.

Do not be that parent. You would never let a three-year-old run into traffic, no matter how hard he cried. Allowing a child to not perform at his academic best is the same as allowing him to run into traffic. You should have the same level of fear and strength in your enforcement with your children's grades.

This is all about their future and giving them the best possible choices for college in case they choose that path. Yes, you should be very concerned about a fourth grader's grades for this reason.

There is no area more important in which you need to be your children's supportive mentor. Guide them down the path to academic excellence.

Help your children find a healthy balance between academic excellence and extracurricular activities. Both are incredibly important to their future.

Some of my most important life lessons and social skills were learned in little league, school clubs, and by playing outside with groups of kids from the neighborhood.

In today's virtual world, it is vital that through high school, children have extracurricular activities where they are physically with others. When I was young, there was no other option, and I am glad for that. Help your child find non-Internet-based social interaction throughout their lives where they are face-to-face with others.

To continue reading on this topic in more detail, please turn to the Foxhole Father chapter, "School/Activities – You are the Main Educator of Your Children," page 115 This QAG section flows into that chapter.

QAG 21 HELPING YOUR TEEN
WITH THE COLLEGE PROCESS

Make sure you read QAG 20 prior to reading QAG 21.

College planning starts once a child is born. Discussions about college should be part of your parenting from the earliest ages.

The first and most important way you can help your children with the college process is to make sure they achieve the best possible grades from the earliest years in school. This is by far one of the most important things you can do for your children.

When they are in high school, they may have to take the SAT or other standardized tests. These tests are used by almost every college acceptance system. I strongly urge enrolling your child in an SAT prep course AND buying other study guides. I bought copies of prior tests to be used at home for extra studying along with the SAT prep course materials.

SAT Prep should start at least six months before your child actually sits for the exam.

Have your child take the prior tests at home under exam conditions. Grade those exams and determine the areas in which your child is weakest. Focus study times on these areas immediately.

Test, test, and retest. What does this do? This will make your child comfortable with the exam format. Making them familiar with what the test experience will be like will increase their scores by itself. If you help them increase their SAT scores, this can mean being considered by better schools. Some colleges have minimum SAT requirements.

Yes, it is a harsh reality, but the world is extremely competitive, and many parents fail their children when it comes to their academic lives. Waiting until someone is a senior in high school is much too late.

From the moment my first child was born, my mission became giving her the best possible chance at attending the college of her choice. I suggest you take the same approach. So many children do not reach their full academic potential because their parents have not prepared them. In their defense, many parents do not know what to do. But perhaps you now know more than you did before you started reading this book.

When your children start high school, plan some college visits. Most institutions have guided tours throughout the year. Don't wait until your child's junior year of high school. So as not to overwhelm them, consider scheduling some college tours during each year of high school.

Stress that going to an in-state college will be less expensive than traveling out of state.

Speak to a CPA about the tax benefits of college savings plans.

Far too many children take generic college majors. Guide your children toward specific majors that will give them skills that will be needed when they graduate. Research professional trends in the business, academic, and medical fields: accounting, computer science, engineering, teaching, nursing, law.

Along these lines, request job placement information for all majors from prospective colleges. Review them with your child. This can really be an eye opener.

Before they are out of grammar school, research what experts believe to be the trades and professions that will be in high demand and best paying in the future. Your ideas of jobs that can support a family may be antiquated. I know mine were. Some of these may not require a college degree.

Parents can become so fixated on their children attending college that they ignore opportunities in trades and vocations that do not require college. Your child's time may be best spent pursuing a career with no college requirement. Many provide the means to financially support themselves and give them a love of their work forever.

There are substantial benefits to joining the military. Most parents' views on this are antiquated. Be open minded and objectively research the current options for a career in all branches of the armed forces.

Your child may have a strong desire to pursue a profession that will not provide the salary needed to live comfortably. Teach her that supporting herself in the future should be her first priority, and that she should pursue a profession that will allow this and fulfill her personally at the same time. Degrees that lead to professional licenses can give your children great social and financial advantages. College is different than lower grades. Children have much more autonomy. However, guide your children to complete a four-year degree in four years or less. To save money, consider summer or winter break courses at a local community college, making sure ahead of time that your child's main college will accept those courses as actual credits within their major and not as electives. The price per credit at a community college can be much less expensive. Every dollar saved on credits earned this way means one less student loan dollar your child will have to pay back later.

OAG 22 PINK HAIR! HEAVY MAKEUP! RIPPED JEANS!

At all times, respect your child as an individual and never make things about you and your feelings. Never mock or use judgmental language.

Many teenagers, at one time or another, may want to express themselves in ways their parents don't approve of.

This could be through clothing, makeup, accessories, music, or habits.

When this happens I would like you to take moment and pause before you have a harsh or judgmental reaction. These types of expression are often because your children are taking control of their own world. These are very important traits to foster within your children. Try to realize that for their entire lives they have been told how to dress and how to look. It makes perfect sense that they will want to take control of their looks at some point.

If what your child wants to do will have long term physical effects, like tattoos or scarring from large piercings, strongly describe the severe, negative long-term consequences. If they will not have long-term physical effects, then try to be supportive and allow these decisions to play out naturally within your children.

This is very hard for many parents, and it was extremely hard for me, but I realized that pink hair never hurt anyone.

It is during these times, when a teenager is trying to find his or her way, that the greatest bonds can be forged between the two of you.

So, yes, give advice, and explain potential negative impacts they may face with their choices. That is always your job as a parent. If you feel they are putting themselves in harm's way physically, then do all you can to stop the behavior in a way that teaches and guides and does not demean them.

When it comes to provocative and revealing clothing, the discussion needs to focus on the importance of modesty and that dressing in a sexually provocative or revealing way is always meant to gain social attention. They should know that seeking attention should never be a motivation for any behavior.

Teach them that they should never dress or accessorize in ways that distract others or bring heightened attention to themselves. This can change based on venue. Being a walking distraction is rude and invades others' space and can ruin their enjoyment.

From when they were very young, if you taught them that acceptance and attention from those around them, including you, should never matter, then you may have fewer instances in which your children want to dress or express themselves solely to stand out in a crowd.

Teach them that wanting to stand out in a crowd by dressing differently, wearing extreme makeup or hair color, or wearing provocative clothing, usually stems from a personal weakness.

Teach your children these things from their earliest moments.

Then take your child to the store to buy that pink hair dye.

OAG 23 FOXHOLE SINGLE FATHER
IF YOUR EX IS HOSTILE

How you interact with your ex will dramatically impact how your children experience the divorce or separation. You can only control yourself, so no matter what the history with their mother, or what situations arise with her, never be angry, aggressive, or abusive toward her, especially in front of your children.

Trust me; this is not easy. I sometimes failed miserably at this.

Always strive for harmony and respectful co-parenting with your children's mother. Some of you may have an ex who is hostile. You have the right and obligation to maintain peace in your personal space and your home.

Even in the most peaceful situations, there is rarely a need to verbally communicate with your ex. This is one of the most common mistakes that separated couples make. When your ex is hostile, verbal communication can be fraught with emotional triggers for both of you, and it can waste your time. The majority of daily information exchange can quickly and easily be done with email. You do not need to text or use the telephone.

The main reason why this is so important is that people are much less venomous when writing an email than they are on the phone.

Unless there is an emergency, there is very little need for you to have communication with their mother during your parenting time. Have confidence that you can take care of your children on your own. Your home environment does NOT include your ex. You should do all you can to limit her imposing her parenting on the functioning of your home.

Also, this makes clear the limits and boundaries you are going to enforce in your personal space.

You do NOT have to talk to her on the telephone.

You do NOT have to have conversations via texting with her.

These recommendations are not based in anger or spite. This guidance will help you create a peaceful new home and life environment based on your parenting vision, and with your rules in place that must be followed.

If your ex is hostile, then during the transfer of the children is NEVER a time to have a discussion. Again, emails can be sent with any notes or information that either of you may need to share.

If your ex wants to use the exchange of the children to ambush and attack you, never respond in any way. Ignore the attack and leave as soon as possible. Remain completely silent.

If your request to have silent exchanges is ignored, simply wear headphones and listen to music during the entire exchange.

You should always maintain your silent exchange rule when things are adversarial.

Again, when your children are in your care, you have the right to completely control that environment and what happens within it.

One final word on this. Never stop your children's mother and your children from communicating, no matter what personal issues you and your ex may have.

Your children need both of you, every day.

OAG 24 FOXHOLE SINGLE FATHER
DOES YOUR EX HAVE A DIFFERENT
PARENTING STYLE?

There are probably many reasons why your relationship with your child's mother did not work out. It is to be expected that you will have different parenting styles—sometimes quite different—from each other.

You have to realize that although you are not physically living with their mother, you can still have a great influence over what happens when your children are with her.

You have every right to discuss what happens in their mother's home. Just as you would help your children understand other environments, school, work, etc., you should help your children navigate and understand their mother's home and parenting style.

If you are raising your children the Foxhole Father way, your influence will be felt in their mother's home. You will always be present in your children's minds and hearts and in their decision-making process. Also, even though you are not with them, they will carry your calm perspectives and example wherever they are.

Everywhere your children are—school, activities, play dates—you have equal rights to dictate what is acceptable for your children. Your input should be welcomed.

You should not dwell on the fact that your children's mother may be leading them in directions you do not approve of. Remember, she is just as important as you, and she has the right, just as you do, to raise her children in the ways that she deems appropriate.

But, at the same time, you should always express your opinion about how anyone is influencing or interacting with your child, even their mother. Your job, especially as a single father, is to help your children navigate and understand all aspects of their lives and relationships. This includes discussing your differences in parenting styles.

It is never OK to discuss the personal issues you have with your ex with your children. They should never be subjected to that. They should never hear about any past differences, arguments, or reasons for your breakup. You should never use the exchange of children as a time to discuss substantial parenting issues with your ex. The transfer of children can include light conversations. Strive to make those moments as positive as possible, as these are the rare moments your children will see you physically together, and they will notice everything. Having sincere, kind, and respectful light conversations with their mother during these times can promote healing and calmness in your children.

Your children should never hear significant discussions between you and their mother. This is a great mistake so many parents make. Children hear everything, especially harsh words and attitudes. Wait until they are asleep to make those calls, or move yourself out of earshot so they cannot hear the conversation. Better yet, use email, especially for volatile topics.

To be honest, as a single father, I have made many mistakes. I have acted very immaturely at times and not always in my children's best interest. I am trying to help you avoid the same mistakes that I have made.

Teaching your children by example is always the best type of parenting. Teaching them to respect their mother and her rules, even when you don't agree with them, is a very significant life lesson for you to impart.

But, at the same time, you have the right, and most importantly the obligation, to help them interpret all aspects of their lives, including the parenting of their mother, if you feel it is necessary.

They should feel comfortable, in both homes, expressing any concerns they have about what their parents are doing.

OAG 25 FOXHOLE SINGLE FATHER - DEALING WITH ANGER TOWARD YOUR EX

Anger is always destructive; patience is always edifying.

You may have left your partner to try to bring peace and emotional health to your family. Even if she left you, that should still be your goal. So, let's make that happen.

If you have anger toward your ex, make it a daily mission to eliminate this from your emotional system. Your children will feel your anger, no matter how you try to conceal it. This may only continue any trauma they experienced when you were living with their mother.

No matter what drama you and their mother went through, try your best to eliminate its impact on your emotional system. It does not matter if she cheated on you with your best friend. Maintaining anger and continued resentment are like giving your family cancer. The children will see it, and it will hurt them.

This is such an important step you can take as a single parent. Why? You are the example of what a man should be in your children's eyes. Getting past your prior relationship issues and finding new happiness is a great life lesson. Your daughters will look romantically toward a man like you, and your sons will try to emulate you.

Be the father that your children deserve. Visualize the attributes of that man and work to become him as hard as you can every day.

If you are not truly happy and are harboring resentments and anger toward your ex, I urge you to immediately seek out a mental health professional who specializes in the trauma experienced by men after a separation from a significant other.

I know these emotional issues are so deep and so hard to get past. All we can do is our deliberate and focused best every day for our kids. If you do that, you are a successful father.

The Foxhole Father is not impacted emotionally by things outside of himself.

When the Foxhole Father falters, he forgives himself, learns from it, eliminates any guilty feelings, and tries his best in the next moment.

That is what I do every day.

SECTION 2

FOXHOLE FATHER

FOXHOLE FATHER

TABLE OF CONTENTS

TALKING TO CHILDREN -
THE BASIC FOXHOLE FATHER PHILOSOPHY

The basic Foxhole Father philosophy starts with becoming the masculine nonjudgmental sanctuary for your children. This should be the basis for your fathering.

This leads to communicating with your children in very deliberate ways.

Throughout this book, I will explain what this means.

Your children will face life choices every day.

Your Foxhole Father mission is to teach them the life skills to successfully navigate those choices.

Along with their mother, you are the first and most important teacher they will ever have. You are their life's guide. Every interaction with your children must start with absolute respect for them as individuals.

Your children will say or do things that upset you. That is a given. This book will show you how to approach these situations to give your children the best possible outcomes.

When situations arise, listen with respect and objectivity. If you believe they are about to make a decision not in THEIR best interest, express why you believe that. Remember, your reasons should always be based on their best interest. Express them that way. Your advice should never be based on your personal feelings.

You should always acknowledge that you know their best thought process brought them to the choices they are making. You should always acknowledge that they are human just like you, and that they are doing the best they can to navigate their lives.

Most importantly, your interaction with your children at these moments needs to be free of judgments.

Have faith that there are ways to have constructive discussions related to controversial and emotionally charged topics. Much of this is in your hands and in the level of self-control you maintain. If you are truly dedicated, you can become the father your children need and deserve, ever considering the long-term ramifications of even the smallest interaction.

Most fathers feel an overwhelming urgency to have an immediate answer to every question and an immediate solution to every problem. We naturally want problems quickly resolved. Yes, during our evolution, this trait made for a successful cave man, but it is sometimes a terrible trait to have while parenting.

We need to fight this tendency and learn to pause and self-observe.

The Foxhole Father exhibits great self-control.

Once we control our tendency toward instinctive and reactive problem solving, we can begin to parent deliberately.

You have a life's worth of perspectives and insights formed from your accumulated experiences.

These are some of your best parenting tools.

If you use them properly, they can:

1.   help your child better understand situations they are experiencing, and then you can …

2.   detail potential consequences, short- and long-term, that they may not have considered and then …

3.   teach them how their actions may be perceived by the world.

If you don't approach your children the right way, all of the benefits of your life experiences could be ignored by them.

The perspectives and insights, acquired over our lifetimes, form the very fabric of our psychological and emotional being. We can call these our "gut feelings" or "instincts," but they also can be called ingrained personal tendencies and biases.

Why is this important to realize, especially when it comes to parenting?

When we are presented with a child-related issue of any kind, these ingrained personal tendencies and biases are going to rise quickly in our hearts and minds and attempt to guide and filter our parenting. Our inner cave man will want to come out, but we must learn to leave him in his cave!

We need to remember it's not about us, and our parenting instincts derived from our life experience will not necessarily equate to the correct parenting for our children. So, using one of my basic parenting tenets, we should evaluate every situation individually and with an open mind, and base our parenting on what is best for the child. This type of parenting is more difficult and more time consuming.

How so?

Some fathers simply follow their first knee-jerk reactions in all situations. These emotion-based decisions are quick and easy for the father but sometimes harmful for the children. This type of decision making rarely considers the child adequately.

The Foxhole Father will take each parenting moment separately and evaluate it based on what is best for each individual child.

The Foxhole Father is patient, thoughtful and deliberate.

No matter what the situation or topic—romance, grades, sex, or drugs—you should take a systematic approach. You need to understand where your child is within his or her development emotionally, psychologically, and physically. You then must parent that unique child through the situation.

Too often parents react to surface facts and make incorrect assumptions without allowing their children to fully express themselves. These incorrect assumptions are then filtered through the parent's accumulated life experience, the child's best interest is not considered, and parenting decisions are made. We can all see how this can lead to parenting disasters. Many parenting situations are treated one dimensionally and with little planning and forethought about the best possible outcomes.

You never have to make these common mistakes again.

What are the basic steps?

1. Remain calm and respectful; talk in a normal tone; never escalate.
2. Listen to the facts without interruption.
3. Listen to your child's feelings without interruption.
4. Ignore your personal feelings and biases.
5. Never use judgmental or critical language.

6. Filter your fathering through what is best for your child.
7. Suggest solutions.

These steps become more important as the intensity of the parenting situation rises.

Using these steps will teach your children to be independent thinkers.

By approaching them respectfully and without judgment, you will help them learn to be thoughtful and deliberate about their actions and conscious of the ramifications of them.

Your children will begin to see you as their advocate and protector.

Learning and using the steps above could open you and your children to an entirely new relationship.

These concepts are explored in greater detail in the chapters to come.

Intense situations are some of the best teaching moments you will ever have, so don't waste them. We need to make the best parenting impact during these moments. Too often teaching moments are lost to loud voices and high emotions on both sides. By becoming a Foxhole Father, you can break harmful parenting patterns.

Foxhole Father gives you tools to avoid many common parenting pitfalls.

CHILDREN NEED A MASCULINE NONJUDGMENTAL SANCTUARY

A nonjudgmental sanctuary means an emotionally and physically safe place where children are loved, nurtured, guided, and never judged. Creating a masculine nonjudgmental sanctuary fosters closeness, trust, and mutual respect.

With the guidance of this book you can easily provide that sanctuary for them, and you will.

One important step to creating a healthy home environment is to eliminate judgment from your parenting. You have likely heard parents who call their children "stupid" or ask them loud and harsh questions like, "What the hell is wrong with you?" and "Do you think that's a good idea?" These comments judge and attack children, and they have no place in your home.

Many children live in homes where they are "emotionally flinching."

We usually think of flinching in physical terms. Dictionaries define flinching as "making a quick, nervous movement of the face or body as an instinctive reaction to surprise, fear or pain."

Emotional flinching is just as real. This is a term I created to describe when a person has been so emotionally subjugated and verbally abused that they can no longer discuss their personal needs. When children have received judgment, ridicule, and mocking from their parents too often, the relationship becomes adversarial, and the parent is no longer a safe haven. In fact, the children can feel like prisoners in their own home, just waiting for another personal attack. In other words, they are emotionally isolated and emotionally flinching. Homes can become emotional minefields to children.

We need to completely eliminate judgment, harsh words, ridicule, and words of disappointment and mocking. If you do this, your children will see you as an emotional and physical sanctuary. That is what they deserve.

What benefits does this have in the future for your children? At some future time, your children may go through something that frightens them or puts them in danger. They may have an abusive situation with a boyfriend or girlfriend, for example. If you have established the correct emotional environment for your children within your home, they are much more likely to come to you when they are in their greatest need. This trust in confiding in you can only be achieved if you deliberately establish a home environment as I have described here. If you have established an unhealthy emotional environment for your children, they can become "emotional flinchers" around you, and you will probably be the last person they will reach out to when they are in trouble.

So often I have heard parents tell their children that they are a disappointment. Your children cannot disappoint you. That is impossible.

Parental disappointment is one of the most common and most damaging forms of judgment. That sentence is so important that I want you to keep reading it until you understand it and believe it.

The Foxhole Father never tells his children they are a disappointment.

Your children should never feel the need to impress you, or seek your favor and approval. What your children do is not about you at all, and it should never presented as if it is.

So many parents inject their emotional needs and fears into their parenting. This can take the form of parents saying, "If you don't do what I say, you are hurting me," or "You really disappointed me." These are forms of emotional bullying.

When you do this, it reduces you to their emotional level, and you become a peer in their eyes. This can make your child feel personally attacked by you. That is never good when you want to help father them through an intense situation.

When you choose to attack and judge your child, the hopes of having a constructive parental impact may be lost forever. The safe nonjudgmental sanctuary you want to create is gone.

When you parent with abusive tactics, your child may do what you demand, but what life lesson have you taught?

You want to raise children who are capable, strong, and considerate

[handwritten margin note: You can be disappointed in their actions, but not them as a person.]

need to connect this to others
Ultimately life isnt about our
kids. It's about
the body of Christ.
6-1

of others. Focusing on their needs and how their actions can negatively impact THEM always leads to the best possible outcomes. This will lead them to become fully functioning adults. Framing your parenting in terms of their needs, without judgmental words or ridicule, especially regarding heated and controversial subject matter, should always be your goal.

What you project to your children will be imprinted in their emotional systems as normal masculine behavior.

Your children, both boys and girls, will most likely be attracted to romantic partners who are like you. They will emulate your behaviors, both good and bad.

The greatest responsibility you will ever have is the etching of "normal" masculine traits into your children's delicate minds and hearts.

The best part of this for you is that from this moment, you will be empowered to present a deliberate set of masculine traits that you want your children to see as normal and acceptable.

Remove your fear from any immediate situation. You need to be the calm one, the nonjudgmental one. You are there unconditionally and without attack.

If your kids are living with divorce, they may feel isolated and dislocated, and they don't know what their parents are thinking. You need to establish a loving, nurturing, caring, and protective bond, starting now: your masculine nonjudgmental sanctuary.

Loud angry voices do not belong in a sanctuary. Raising your voice to your children is simply a way of expressing YOUR emotions, and there is no place for that. Loud voices from fathers rarely instill good emotional lessons. You can speak directly, be completely understood, and show the seriousness of situations without yelling.

This takes practice for some men, as parenting children correctly takes an incredible amount of time and patience. Most men, like me, want to fix situations quickly and by any means necessary.

When you begin to filter all of your actions through "What is best for my child?" you will quickly self-observe and see how much yelling and other damaging behaviors are hurting your children.

I am not advocating parental permissiveness or a hands-off approach. Quite the contrary.

Children need clear and strict rules, limits, boundaries, and discipline to thrive.

The Foxhole Father NEVER expresses his personal problems to his young or teenage children.

This is so common today. So many parents want to be friends with their children and live vicariously through them. Many parents lack emotional support from adults and look to their children to share their burdens. I believe this is unhealthy for both the parents and children. If you are doing this, find other emotional support for yourself.

Children know when you are relying on them emotionally, and this puts them in a terrible position.

What is that position? Having responsibility for their parent's happiness. This is never their job.

Not wanting to disappoint their parents, children may continue behaviors or extracurricular activities they do not like. This pressure can be immense, and it is selfish of a parent to do that to a child. Children should not have to worry about their parents' emotional state or maintaining it.

The Foxhole Father never relies on his non-adult children for emotional support.

Your emotional needs are your burden to carry, never your children's.

PARENTING FROM A MASCULINE PERSPECTIVE IS OK

You are a male parent with innate masculine sensibilities that are very important to convey to your children. I believe exposing your children to these masculine sensibilities is just as important as exposing them to feminine sensibilities. In my experience with families over the past twenty-five years, I have seen a marginalization of boys and men and the demonization of the word "masculine" and masculine traits, even in toddlers.

Young boys' natural energy levels and developmental needs are now characterized as "disorders" and suppressed with drugs.

Male college enrollment and performance is gravely suffering, yet where is the national outrage at this catastrophe? Unfortunately it is not seen as a catastrophe at all in many circles, as men are seen as optional and sometimes unnecessary.

Even with all of the progress made over the past several decades, fathers are still taught that child rearing is the domain of a mother. Single-parent households have further eroded fathering impacts.

Whether you are living with your children's mother or you are a single father, I hope this book will be a call to action for the rest of your life. I hope it helps you shed the layers of socialized self-doubt that may be suffocating your fatherhood.

Your children need to feel your presence and influence every day in deep and meaningful ways.

I have met so many men who appear lost and out of touch with their true selves and worth.

The definition of the word masculine has been twisted in the media and other circles in recent years. Many people who read this book may initially confuse the meaning of the word masculine with that bastardized definition.

So, completely erase any definition you have for masculine traits and let's build a new one together and live it.

Masculine traits are positive traits.

The following are NOT masculine traits:

- Negative aggressive and loud behavior
- Misogynistic behavior
- Lack of patience
- Inability to nurture
- Inability to focus
- Allowing fear to stop you from doing the right thing
- Acting macho (blatant outward expressions of "male" behavior)
- Insensitivity to others' emotional needs

The following are masculine traits:

- Physically protecting yourself
- Positive aggressive and loud behavior
- Having patience
- Nurturing
- Ability to focus and stay on task
- Understated demeanor
- Respect for women
- Knowing right from wrong
- Doing the right thing at all times, regardless of fear
- Wanting to provide for your family
- Wanting to maintain a safe environment for your family
- Sensitivity and consideration of others' needs
- Bonding with other men
- Wanting to take care of a woman and make a home for her

Men and women process information and emotions differently. Often, I have seen men's natural thought processes and emotional processes be questioned or ridiculed, especially when it comes to parenting. I cannot speak to a woman's thought process, and I would never attempt to.

But, men, you don't have to change your natural way of processing information or emotions to be an excellent parent. You should simply use your innate systems to parent successfully.

Masculine traits are needed today more than ever. Your children need exposure to your masculine traits and thought processes as much as they need exposure to their feminine counterparts.

By using the advice in this book, the most masculine or most feminine of people, regardless of gender, can turn their children into functional and happy adults.

The difference between masculine and feminine is most times very subtle. But it is impossible to get either gender to unlearn their inborn emotional and psychological processing, and we should not try.

The Foxhole Father learns what his children need from him and then creates that environment using his inherent masculine traits.

It is very important to note that society's exaggerated externally focused definition of masculinity is NOT what I am talking about here. Nor am I in any way diminishing innate feminine qualities. Today, thankfully, both genders have learned they have both masculine and feminine traits.

This book assumes you are a dedicated father who lives to nurture your children. It is not my place to psychoanalyze you and to try to change anything about your innate systems. I would not disrespect you like that. You are smart and capable of achieving anything you set your mind to. All I am trying to do in this book is to share my field-tested ideas. This field testing started in April 1990 when my first child was born.

Combining Foxhole Fathering concepts with your immense dedication, intelligence, and tenacity allows you to parent with new depth, understanding, and even more clear goals.

So please do not listen to anything you hear that says that masculine traits are a bad thing. This is ridiculous. Our children need masculine traits to be successful in life.

I was born in Queens, New York. I am one of six children, three boys and three girls. It was a traditional Irish-Italian household. The boys were expected to do traditional masculine things and the girls were expected to do traditional feminine things. Anything to do with babies was foreign to me. I was supposed to be outside shoveling snow or painting the house, and I believed that men could not and should not care for the direct needs of children.

I share this with you to explain that I could not have had less experience with children, or less confidence about taking care of children, when my first child was born. You may be in the same position. But even with this complete lack of knowledge and confidence, my natural and inborn masculine fathering instincts instantly appeared the first moment I held my baby.

Have confidence! If your basis in parenting starts from a masculine nonjudgmental place, your parenting will be a complete success.

You don't need to change your basic masculine nature at all.

Filter your desire to be a good parent through it.

BE THE MAN YOUR CHILDREN NEED

The man your children need can shift from minute to minute. As a father you need to drop the thought that only your traditional masculine traits and masculine roles are going to be needed. If you don't, your children will only be 50% complete.

In every moment, the man you are should flow from your children's immediate needs.

I quickly learned that there are no masculine or feminine parenting jobs. There are only children's needs that must be addressed.

Singing lullabies, softly putting Band-Aids on boo-boos, sewing a button back on a winter coat so carefully that no one can tell it was ever detached, and accepting a face full of makeup are just a few things men need to embrace for the betterment of their children.

If you get past any hang-ups, playing all roles and being a father who will do whatever it takes to nurture his children in any moment becomes easy and a true joy.

If you find you are embarrassed doing certain things that you have been taught are not masculine, or not "men's work," remember that you want your children to ignore what society says are acceptable gender roles, so you need to start doing the same.

Your children's needs should dictate the father you give them. Your behavior should not be driven by societal definitions of manhood.

SHOULD I EVER HIT MY CHILDREN?

No, you should never hit your children.

One of the first decisions I made as a father was to never raise a violent hand to my children under any circumstances. A Foxhole Father provides a safe place for his children, while maintaining limits, boundaries, and rules meant to form them into fully functional adults.

Let's take a moment and look at the emotions at play when we hit our children.

When a child is behaving in a way that we don't approve of, we want them to stop that behavior. When loud words and threats do not work for us, we sometimes escalate and get physically violent as a means to make them stop.

You love your children and you tell them so, hopefully often. What lesson are you teaching the five-year-old child you are hitting/assaulting? You are teaching her that it is acceptable for the rest of her life that someone who says he loves her in one moment can strike her in the next.

Do you want your child to grow up believing that physical abuse is part of a loving relationship? Of course not. If you hit your children, what else are they to believe?

Imagine we are talking about daughters specifically for a moment. Do you want your daughters to be comfortable being hit by a man as part of a loving relationship? If you hit your daughters, it is possible they will accept physical abuse from a man who supposedly loves them.

Conversely, do you want your children to believe that they should use physical abuse to control others throughout their lives?

Physical abuse, and yes, I put spanking under this heading, will lead to children who flinch from you and who will fear you. Children who are hit do not see their parents as their safe haven, but instead see them as a minefield they need to navigate through every day. Can you imagine the stress an eight-year-old is under knowing a two-hundred-pound adult can hit him at any moment?

Children I have seen who are consistently hit sometimes become reclusive, secretive, and immature teenagers. Sometimes they become violent bullies.

Eliminating physical violence from your parenting does force you to take more time and to deal with more stress. But this is much better than the alternative, especially for a child's emotional development. If you hit your small child and he stops a behavior, that does nothing to properly prepare that child for life. He doesn't have the mental capacity to process such physical actions against him, nor should he ever. This is not the type of teaching moment you want for your children.

Always, the entire focus should be, "What is best for the children?" Many times it is best to stop children from behaving in a certain way, and we can achieve this without striking them.

There are other alternatives, and one good example is a time-out, and when necessary, a forced time-out.

There are times when you may have to physically stop your child from behaving in a certain manner, such as when a three-year-old wants to run in the street. When calm discussion from you does not work and your child will not stop a behavior, you may need to hold your child in a time-out.

When they have calmed down later, take the time to explain why you needed to stop them from whatever it was they were doing.

Teaching children self-control and impulse-control is one of your main goals as a Foxhole Father. It is in your children's best interest if you instill these in them as soon as possible.

This can be done without violently striking them. My three daughters, all functioning adults now, prove that.

In the long run, hitting children teaches them the following regressive life lessons:

- Being assaulted by a loved one is acceptable.
- Controlling those you love by physical force is acceptable.

Don't ever hit your children.

LIMITS, BOUNDARIES, AND RULES

My three children have thrived because I instituted limits, boundaries, and rules.

There are two main points in this chapter that go hand in hand:

1. Limits, boundaries, and rules are the main building blocks of functioning adults.
2. Reward only behaviors that you want your children to repeat. Children will continue behaviors that give them the results they want. It is simple but true. You have to be careful which behaviors you reward.

I am not talking about being a dictator or making your children so fearful that they do what you tell them to. My fathering style is quite the opposite, and yours should be as well.

Children need structure, and they need to understand why you are giving them certain limits and boundaries. Yes, this takes time and energy, but the more you communicate with them the underlying reasons for your parenting decisions, the more likely you are to have calm and loving discussions in their teenage and later years.

Many parents will say, "Just because I said so." There is, of course, a time and place for that, and not all decisions that parents make need to be fully explained to children. There is not always time. But most times, even with the smallest child who can hear and understand you, you need to take the time to explain why you have made a rule or are putting a limit on them or giving them a boundary.

Setting limits, boundaries, and rules, like all of your fathering decisions, should be filtered through what is best for your children. If you are an active father, you will make many unpopular decisions. Your children may perceive you as mean, and many times they will express anger toward you. You must never buckle under to these emotional attacks. You need to be emotionally above the discussions. If you are no longer in a relationship with your children's mother, and she was abusive toward you, these angry outbursts from your children can easily bring you back to terrible moments you have experienced in your old home.

This can lead you to have an extreme emotional and verbal reaction toward your children. You can never allow your past experiences to impact your fathering that way. Having confidence that setting limits and boundaries, no matter how much friction it causes, is critical to creating fully functioning adults.

If you find you cannot control your emotions and that you are getting upset and attacking your child, you must seek professional help for this immediately. Having emotional outbursts and loudly arguing with your children is never the behavior you want to show them. Remember, you want to be the masculine and nonjudgmental place. You want to be their sanctuary.

Setting limits, boundaries, and rules will instill self-control and impulse-control, two of the most important attributes your children will need to be successful in life. I cannot stress this enough. The permissive father who wants to avoid parenting friction often raises children who are mentally weak or arrogant, who impose on others, and who have a delayed adulthood. The father who glorifies everything his children do and refuses to firmly guide them does the greatest disservice imaginable.

You are not their friend. Friendship with your children will hopefully come much later. You are in the process of forming and nurturing fully functioning adults. That is always your goal. It is in their best interest for you to be their father first in all situations. That is what they need.

As I discuss throughout this book, your children should know that every decision you make, no matter how unpopular with them, is filtered through "what is best for them." If you want them to eat their dinner, go to bed at a certain hour, not maintain a friendship with someone you deem unacceptable, follow a curfew, etc., tell them how these decisions are best for them.

A good way to view how resolute you should be when making limits, boundaries, and rules is to remember when your child was three years old and wanted to run into the street. You would never allow a child to run into traffic no matter how much he fought you. No matter how elaborate his tantrum, of course he could not be allowed to run into the street. You would even risk your own life to prevent this from happening.

As your children get older, you need to have the same emotional strength and conviction with rules you make. So when a fourteen-year-old wants to sleep at a friend's house whose parents you have never met, think of how strong you were when he wanted to run into street. No matter what reaction that fourteen-year-old has, no matter what threats he makes, and, of course, when he screams, "I will hate you forever if you don't let me go!", remain calm and unmoving, and never allow yourself to escalate along with him.

If you believe that setting a limit, boundary, or rule is in their best interest, NEVER buckle under to any pressure. Remember, that would be like allowing a three-year-old to run into traffic.

THE POWER OF PAUSING

When a situation gets me emotionally upset, I have found pausing to be a great strategy. This sounds like a very simple concept, and it is.

I have found that pausing helps to:

- Stop the escalation of emotions and loud voices
- Provide a silent time that gives everyone a chance to breathe and calm down
- Stop me from attacking my child and get back into objective fathering mode sooner
- Temper my inborn masculine need to defuse situations immediately and aggressively

A very good friend and mentor of mine, George Rademacher, taught me the power of pausing.

When I was younger, I would rarely take a moment to deliberately think about what I was going to say or do when a volatile situation arose.

This caused so many problems. It delayed the resolution of issues with family members and other people I care about. Once I mastered this simple lesson, it helped me in all areas of my life.

What does pausing mean to a Foxhole Father?

It means to always take a moment to gather your thoughts and collect yourself before responding to any situation, especially one that may be emotionally charged with your children.

There are so many times, especially when children are young, when we are emotionally strained and tired, and it is very easy to raise our voices and say harsh words. This is never how we want to represent ourselves to our children. Remember, you're supposed to be the masculine nonjudgmental sanctuary for them. That means, at all times and in all situations, striving to be calm and respectful toward them, no matter how they are acting toward us.

As I describe in a prior chapter ("Children Need a Masculine Nonjudgmental Sanctuary" pp #), emotional flinching is real.

When you verbally attack your children, this can make them emotionally flinch away from you.

If you raise your voice and use harsh words and body language, your children will learn to fear you.

It is so common to have loud and harsh reactions, and believe me, I have been guilty of this with my own children. But with some practice and with self-observation, you can overcome this knee-jerk reaction and become a much more effective parent. Once a pattern of emotional flinching is established within your children, it is very difficult to undo that damage.

So, from the very outset of your parenting life, be the nonjudgmental masculine sanctuary for them. Never become a monster within their home who they are afraid of emotionally or physically.

A good way to prevent this is to use the power of pausing.

INDEX OF EXPECTED BEHAVIORS

Quite often we maintain an index of expected behaviors for people in our lives. This index can vary depending on what position in our lives a person holds. These are not consciously created by us, but imprinted within us in various ways from the day we were born. These indexes are not based on our true needs, but are one dimensional, absolute rules not to be broken.

For example, we may believe our mothers must send us a birthday card or make us a birthday cake.

We may expect that our brother will fix our fence for free because he owns a fence company.

We may expect our children to dress like us, or to give us a present on Father's Day.

We may expect our daughters to never wear makeup, or we may expect them to take dance or gymnastics or compete in cheerleading.

We may expect others to express love the same way that we do.

We may blindly expect and demand that our children be heterosexual.

My advice is to dismantle any index of expected behaviors you have inside of you.

It is impossible for anyone to live up to these arbitrary sets of rules. And they should not have to.

Maintaining such indexes can only lead to certain disappointment and emotional distance in your relationships.

Maybe you have been the victim of this? Do you have someone in your life who is telling you that because of your specific relationship to them that there are certain things you must or mustn't do?

Or maybe you are inflicting this type of dysfunction on those around you? On your children?

You should allow people to love and share with you in ways that come naturally to them. Telling someone what their expected behaviors are is never a good idea. Being open to accepting love from others on their terms can also be a wonderful life lesson for us. But, if many of your needs aren't being met, you may need to walk away.

Telling someone that he or she is not living up to your index of expected behaviors can be extremely painful for that person. Most people in our lives are doing the best they can. They cannot be perfect.

The following comments illustrate someone who is dictating to others how they should feel or act through his or her set index:

- "If you loved me, you would …"
- "You're my wife, so you should always …"
- "My sons will play football …"
- "You're my father, so you have to …"
- "You will get married in a church …"

I have explained this thought process to my daughters in an effort to open their minds and help them better understand their own actions. I wanted them to be able to recognize when someone is applying an index of expected behaviors to them.

How could this apply to your romantic relationship?

You may have chosen a partner not based on a romantic love at all. In reality you may have chosen her because she meets your index of expected behaviors and attributes perfectly. Sometimes people choose friends and partners this way, with no consideration of emotions as the basis for the decision.

How does this apply to fathering?

You may have an index of expected behaviors for your children. Many of these can be the usual aspirations: college, athletics, marriage, etc. Many of these can be in your child's best interest, and some may not.

Some parents may push their children into extracurricular activities their children may not like. Some parents live vicariously through their children.

If you believe something is in your child's best interest, you may have to push a reluctant child into that behavior. This happens all of the time.

Are you being forceful and unmoving about your child's need to dress a certain way or participate in an activity? Take some time to pause and objectively analyze your parenting. Is it based on an index of expected behaviors you have? Is there any deep thought behind your expectation? Are you living vicariously?

What if your child questions your demand that they participate in something? If you can't clearly explain why it is in their best interest and find yourself saying things like, "You need to do this because I had to do it when I was brought up," or "Just because you're supposed to," or "I want you to," then I would pause, self-observe, and start the thought process about this activity from scratch, using the tools outlined in this book.

A good example of a parent demanding his children excel at something because it is in their best interest to do so is academics.

In the days to come, try to see if you are guilty of maintaining an index of expected behaviors with one or more people in your life. Is this causing friction and arguments? Are you consistently disappointed in certain relationships? Why are you maintaining them? Are you taking responsibility for your equal share of the blame?

Imagine how this can help your children have healthier and more fulfilling relationships throughout their entire lives. Understanding and being aware of our own personal indexes, and knowing others have their own, sets us apart.

It brings control of our happiness inside of us, instead of allowing things outside of us to impact our feelings.

This helps me every day in all of my relationships, both business and personal.

INTENTIONS SPEAK LOUDER THAN BEHAVIORS

I have taken the liberty of changing an old adage we all know so well. I felt it needed a little updating after all of these centuries.

So, yes, behaviors speak louder than words, but I believe that

Intentions Speak Louder Than Behaviors.

I am going to use a common parent-child conflict to explain this notion. As I go through my example, I want you to think about how you approach similar situations with your children. This can be about the clothes they wear, the color of their hair, their choice of friends, or the books they are reading, etc.

The goal of this chapter is to show that the intentions and the emotions driving decisions are the most significant part of any discussion with a child about their behavior, especially a teenager. Many intense parenting situations appear to us suddenly and without warning. We must be ever aware of this so we can temper our initial reactions. Controlling and being deliberate about your parenting reactions is one of the most important gifts you could ever give your child.

Imagine that one day, your clean-cut son comes home, looking a bit different. You are suddenly confronted with this situation.

Artist Credit Leo Palmer FRPS FPSA

He is wearing lipstick and heavy eye makeup, a dog collar and leash, and, in your opinion, outrageous clothes.

You may have had the same reaction as his father below.

Image courtesy of imagerymajestic at FreeDigitalPhotos.net

I think it is very apparent what is happening here with the people pictured.

I call them "Timmy" and "The Father."

We have all had, or have, the same feelings this father is experiencing. And I am sure that our children have felt exactly how Timmy is feeling right about now as well.

But first, before I go on, I would like you to do an exercise.

1. Self-observe and try to determine your core feelings about what Timmy has done. Think of a parenting situation in which you were actually confronted with a child's behavior that shocked you. What were your initial feelings and reactions? This is extremely significant, as these core unfiltered feelings quite often drive our parenting reactions. Using these initial and unfiltered emotions to parent your child is quite often a terrible mistake.
2. Think of what you might initially say to Timmy and how you might say it.

It is important to be honest here.

•   What would be the level of your voice?

- What words would you use to discuss this?
- Would you even be able to "discuss" this?
- Would you use words of judgment? Of mocking?
- Would you ask leading questions?

Let's move on and explore this situation a little deeper. Let's look at the father's side of this "problem."

There are so many possible emotions that parents feel at these moments, and there are almost always multiple emotions at play. Right? This could be a conflict over music, who your children choose to be friends with, alcohol or drug use, lack of interest in school work, the color of your child's hair, or the clothes he is wearing. The possibilities are endless.

But the core issue is simple; your child has done something you don't like or approve of. What are some of the feelings we may have as parents? Embarrassment? Sure, many parents would feel embarrassed being seen in public with Timmy or knowing he is going to school each day wearing makeup and dressed that way. Outrage? Sure, at the disrespect Timmy is showing you by engaging in behaviors you do not approve of. Shock? Of course, to see such a radical transformation in your son's appearance.

I leave the most common one for last:

FEAR. Timmy's look can evoke fear on many levels, some we can't really put our finger on, right? We may actually fear him, as well as be afraid for him.

Most times, the parental reaction includes a judgment about the character of the child and loud and harsh language when the parents are afraid and frustrated. It is these two things, words of judgment and harsh language, that should be avoided, because the use of these can only serve to alienate your child further.

For example, avoid saying things like:

- "What is wrong with you?"
- "You are so stupid!"
- "You look like a freak!"
- "You are an embarrassment to me! I can't be seen with you!"

Even though we have all felt these things, they are NEVER going to help teach your children anything positive. Again, these types of comments should be avoided at all costs.

Let me go back to the theme of this chapter:

Intentions Speak Louder Than Behaviors.

I want you to ponder this again in the context of my discussion above. The Foxhole Father never overreacts to or demonizes behaviors that could one day be normal for his child. I did not always succeed in controlling my initial reactions, and I failed my children many times with the way I initially parented them in certain situations.

In the case of Timmy, although it may look extreme to us, in some teenaged circles it is accepted. This is not to say that what Timmy has done is good for him. I am just trying to give you a broader perspective and context on his behavior.

Many parents react to discussions about sex, drugs and alcohol, and clothing choices in ways that push children away. But these are the areas in which our kids need the most nurturing, nonjudgmental, and calm places to discuss their choices and feelings.

You can be that place for the rest of their lives. Let me restate my thoughts here.

The Foxhole Father never overreacts to or demonizes behaviors that one day could be normal or that will not leave lasting physical marks on their bodies.

So, pink hair? Fine …

But a large metal bar through the eyebrow that will leave a permanent and very visible scar for the rest of their lives? Or a tattoo that they may eventually regret? I would do all that I could to show them what the long lasting and sometimes permanent negative impact could be from such choices.

I want to give you some personal background on myself and my kids. Since my divorce in 1997, I have had equal physical custody of my children. They were six, five, and three years old. My time with my children included all of the Fridays and Saturdays.

Why do I tell you this? Most after-school social interaction and emotional development occurs on Fridays and Saturdays. I personally had to manage my children's social lives, from preschool playdates to movie pickups to teenage car dates, and everything in between. I had to manage who they were allowed to socialize with and which parents I found suitable for them to be around.

I know what it's like to have clothing, makeup, and curfew negotiations.

I mention this only to show that my parenting advice and philosophy come from being in the trenches, day in and day out, and physically and emotionally parenting my children in the most significant parts of their lives, not from some theoretical philosophy.

All of these fathering moments were gifts to me. All the times my children confided in me or asked my advice, especially as teenagers, showed me I was on the right track.

I let my kids express their opinions, and then I gave advice I thought would work for THEM.

Remember, when in need, you want your children to always come to you. If your children discuss things with you, that needs to be nurtured always, no matter how upsetting the topic is to you.

Remember the Power of Pausing.

They don't have to talk to you. They don't have to confide in you. You must show your children as often as possible that you are their nonjudgmental sanctuary.

Although I discuss many things with my children, I am not a permissive parent at all. I believe in strict limits, boundaries, and rules, and I believe that children flourish when they have them. Having nonjudgmental nurturing discussions along with strict limits, boundaries, and rules will help your children grow into functional adults.

I want you to meet Timmy again.

Many parents ask their children questions like, "Timmy, do you think that is a good idea?" or "You aren't going out looking like that, are you?" as their kids are walking out the door.

Imagine as you were leaving for work, someone asked you, "You aren't going out looking like that, are you?" Wouldn't that be disturbing to you? Yes, it would.

Remember, we all think our ideas are great ideas and that how we are dressed is acceptable.

So, look at Timmy and remember that everything he is doing, he believes is a great idea—and probably the best idea of all time.

Asking those types of questions are insults and mocking. We should not be asking these types of questions of anyone at any age.

There is nothing I dislike more than someone asking, "Hey, Chris, do you really think that's a good idea?"

When we ask this, we are basically calling the person STUPID. It is not a good idea to mock a child. If you are Timmy's parents and you are concerned, you need to carefully phrase your questions to teach him something, not ridicule him.

Try to find an alternative to "Do you think that's a good idea?" If you are actually concerned about negative consequences for someone, then express that loving thought constructively.

Your embarrassment should not be part of the conversation, at least not now. Is Timmy's behavior or his clothes really bad for Timmy? It could be true that they are. The Foxhole Father needs to focus on helping his child understand all possible negative consequences for that child. And we cannot begin to teach them anything until we understand their intentions, right?

Because?

Intentions Speak Louder Than Behaviors.

I am going to lay out two scenarios about the intentions behind Timmy's behavior and then discuss my thoughts about them.

We see two children with identical outward appearances. How would a Foxhole Father start the discussion with Timmy 1 and Timmy 2? The same way for each of them.

Please meet Timmy 1 and Timmy 2.

My fathering starts out identically. Like this:

With both Timmys, I start off by telling him that I love him and I live to take care of him. I tell him that I want him to have the best chances at life. I also tell him that he has every right to dress however he wants. I am honest about my initial feelings, and I tell him that his heavy makeup and how he dresses alarms me, but I am not judging him, just discussing my initial feelings and reactions. I tell him, as always, my initial personal feelings have no place in this discussion. I ask him to talk to me about his sudden change in appearance. I tell him I really want to understand this, and that my concerns are only for him.

I respect Timmy, don't preach or condescend to him, and that leads how I frame the discussion we are having.

I tell him that although it is wrong, people can judge us on our outward appearance and that can eventually lead to important opportunities being missed.

That is my greatest concern, that although he has every right to dress how he wishes, there may be a personal price to pay that may not be worth it.

More importantly than how Timmy is dressed, I really want to understand his motivation or his intentions.

I explain that most behaviors are not good or bad, but we need to look at our intentions to see if they are good for us and emotionally healthy.

Timmy 1 opens up …

Timmy 1 starts to explain that his "crowd" dresses this way, and the heavy makeup is part of the dress code.

That is a very normal thing to say. Let's look at ourselves for a moment. Don't we dress how our "crowd" dresses? In our places of business, we adhere to a dress code. Out socially, we adhere to dress codes. If we are a member of the military, belong to a club or bowling league, aren't we expected to adhere to dress codes? Of course, we are constantly allowing society and our business and social circles to dictate how we dress.

Yes, we dress different from Timmy 1, but Timmy 1 has a different crowd than we do. He is simply mirroring behavior that his parents demonstrate as important every day, conforming to dress codes.

Timmy 1 goes on, though, and you can see he feels incredible pressure to maintain this look for fear of being pushed out of the crowd.

This is a great opening to discuss broader life issues with Timmy 1, peer pressure and being a leader, not a follower, for example. This is a good time for discussions about how in this situation, HIS needs are not being met. He is acting under desperation and fear, and those are NEVER good motivations. You see, we are not saying the behavior is wrong at all, because it is not necessarily wrong. But the intentions can come from a weak place and an insecure place. That is bad for Timmy 1.

So with Timmy 1, he needs guidance and understanding to help him gain the strength to be his own person and not live his life behaving how the crowd behaves for fear of being exiled. He is facing intense pressure out in the world to conform, and he needs his Foxhole Father to help him figure it all out. Now is not the time to attack Timmy 1.

It is your job to provide that nonjudgmental sanctuary for Timmy 1.

Timmy 2 opens up …

Just like Timmy 1, he starts to explain that his "crowd" dresses this way, and the heavy makeup is part of the dress code.

Yes, we dress different from Timmy 2, but Timmy 2 has a different crowd than we do.

Timmy 2 goes on, though, and you can see that he is dressing as a true part of his current expression at his age. He feels good about it and has confidence about it. In fact, he has led the crowd to dress this way. So his intentions or emotional basis comes from a strong, individual place. He is a leader. His intentions or emotional basis for dressing this way is healthy. The fact that you do not like it does not matter. I know that is hard to hear. So Timmy 2 needs to be told that he is on the right track emotionally, and that you are happy to see his motivations come from inside of him. Timmy 2 is showing great strength of character.

Timmy 2 is creating social standards others are following.

So, let's bring this conversation back to the analogies I used above. If you are following dress codes in your daily life and are not doing this out of insecurity or an emotional weakness, then hopefully you can understand and endorse the basis for what Timmy 2 is doing.

You need to support his intentions underlying his behavior.

The concepts being explained in this example are vital to Foxhole Fatherhood.

But with both Timmy 1 and Timmy 2, you want to emphasize how this behavior or manner of dress can negatively impact them in the broader world.

Even though with Timmy 2 you seem to have instilled strong individual personality traits, the impact on his life may be negative in the long run. If you feel there may be negative impacts, then the conversation should continue with a discussion about these. Make sure he mirrors back those potential negative consequences and understands them.

If this discussion about negative impacts is done without mocking or judgment, then for both Timmy 1 and Timmy 2, this discussion with you can become two things:

1. A fantastic teaching moment that goes well beyond the current situation and
2. A moment when his faith and trust in you as his protector and teacher is solidified.

These are two things we always want to strive for when communicating with our children.

Let's now take a look at your other son, Billy.

Hopefully, we can now take an objective look at him as well. He is the star quarterback, at the top of his class, and he dates the head cheerleader. Billy seems to be perfect, so you usually don't give his emotional state and intentions much thought.

Report Card
A+
A+
A+
A+
A+
A+

But this is a mistake.

Just as we did with Timmy, we need to understand the intentions and motivations behind Billy's actions.

They may not be healthy at all.

Remember, behavior is not bad or good.

What if Billy really hates football?

What if Billy really likes another person in his class who is not the most popular or the most beautiful?

Most fathers would feel incredibly happy with Billy and would feel like their job is done. But Billy may be in a terrible emotional place, just like Timmy 1.

Timmy 2, with facial tattoos, could be totally functional, even though he's doing things you don't like. Whereas Billy, the quarterback, could be doing things you deem acceptable within your index of expected behaviors, but he may not be emotionally healthy and functional at all.

Why is he the quarterback? Why is he clean-cut? Why is he working out? Why is he dating the cheerleader?

There could be many negative emotional reasons for these things to be happening. Behavior is not necessarily bad or good; behavior is not necessarily acceptable or unacceptable. The underlying intentions and motivations that drive behavior need to be understood before we can effectively parent our children.

Timmy or Billy
Who is emotionally healthy?

Behaviors do NOT always tell us the answer.
So, let's go back to the beginning.

I hope your reaction to Timmy is much different than it was when I first showed you these pictures, and your parenting from now on will be much more deliberate.

Children will retract emotionally if you don't handle interactions carefully. The more this happens, the more that distance can grow, and your love and concern may be rendered useless. I know more than anyone how hard parenting can be.

I know how easy it is to raise your voice and use damaging language to get kids to behave, especially when you are frightened for your children.

Just because a child does what you demand does not mean you have taught that child anything but to fear you and become evasive. And that is the worst life lesson a child can learn from a parent.

The Foxhole Father always remembers ...

**INTENTIONS SPEAK
LOUDER THAN BEHAVIORS.**

DESPERATION LEADS TO SELF-COMPROMISE LEADS TO ENSLAVEMENT

If you are impacted by only one concept from this book, the next one would be a good choice.

Learn it, evaluate your own life through it, and then teach it to your children.

DESPERATION leads to
SELF-COMPROMISE leads to
ENSLAVEMENT.

Before I go on, it is important to understand that desperation is much more intense than the average teenage social anxieties I describe in this book. I draw a distinction between the two, but many people do not.

For purposes of this chapter, I am defining desperation as an intense irrational anxiety or overpowering physical urge. Once we act with these as a motivating factor instead of our true best interest and desires at heart, we can quickly become enslaved.

To expand on the concept, desperation (intense irrational anxiety or overpowering physical urge) can lead people to self-compromise (doing things not in their self-interest, and many times harmful), which can lead to enslavement (continuing to do that thing to quell the desperation).

In this chapter, we are talking about desperation for anything. Desperation can impact every area of our lives.

Desperation for sex, money, love, drugs, social status, friends ... the list is endless.

Let's say your child is DESPERATE for social acceptance. This is not just a simple weakness, but a situation where your child is overwhelmed by something he can no longer use rational thought or willpower to avoid doing.

Using your Foxhole Fathering skills in these situations is so important. This does not mean that whenever your child has an interest in doing what others are doing that there is an underlying desperation or emotional weakness; quite the contrary. My teenagers were extremely social, and every day there seemed to be a new fad they were coming home with. Most times, the behaviors that they wanted to mimic were harmless, and their wanting to be part of current trends had no basis in peer pressure or a deep blind need to be accepted socially. There is no desperation attached to the motivations in these cases. There is only a healthy sense of unity, belonging, and shared social experiences within a peer group.

So, it is very important to see the difference. A good way to achieve this is by having loving and open channels of communication at all times in your home. This will help your children feel comfortable expressing themselves to you.

You may have identical twins wanting to do the same exact behavior, and one of them may have a very healthy motivation while the other may be filled with desperation.

Most parents mistakenly label behaviors as good or bad, when in actuality there is no such thing.

The Foxhole Father's job is to understand the underlying motivations of behavior. This is discussed at length in the chapter "Intentions Speak Louder Than Behaviors," page 78.

Your Foxhole Father mission is to gain a much deeper understanding of their psyches and to create leaders. When you find that their motivation has its roots in desperation, the desired behavior or activity is not relevant. The fact that their motivation is coming from a clouded emotional place is highly relevant.

These situations usually begin with you observing a behavior in your child or you denying your child's request for something. Then you hear this in one form or another, usually in a loud voice:

"… but everyone is doing it/wearing it/listening to it … and if I don't, I will look stupid/be embarrassed, have no friends…. "

When a child is desperate for something she is consumed with negative emotions. She can loudly make demands and attack you personally. It is very easy for fathers to get defensive and for things to emotionally and verbally escalate. But try your best to keep a level head and keep your focus and energy on helping her navigate these intense issues.

Are you feeling that the behavior is ultimately bad for your child or that the motivation is unhealthy? Or is it both?

For example, if my child is feeling peer pressure to go skydiving, both the behavior and the motivation are unhealthy or dangerous.

If my child is feeling desperate to dye her hair pink, the behavior is harmless, but the motivation is still unhealthy or dangerous.

It is important to state all things in terms of their lives and the consequences they will have to live with. Nothing can be deemed in your best interest or as your personal preference. These rarely need to be discussed, and they never supersede the best interest of the child. Of course, your preferences may quite often bring the best outcomes for him or her.

I will now get back to the confrontation in which your child is demanding to mimic the current social behavior.

Depending on what the child wants to do, these situations can make us frightened, and when that is coupled with a confrontational attitude, it can be a recipe for a parent exploding verbally at his children. You must avoid allowing your personal feelings to become part of the conversation in this way. Especially if you feel fear or anger, pause, self-observe, and stop yourself from expressing these negative reactions.

In the long run, specific issues or situations are insignificant. Most of these are temporary, like changing hair color. How you handle them may never be forgotten, though, and it may be permanently imprinted in your child's emotional system.

You need to first express that you are glad your child is discussing this with you and not attempting hide it from you (if that is the case).

Your discussion should always focus on how things can impact the children in a negative way. I rarely tell my children that I simply don't approve of something and leave it at that. If you rule with an iron fist, yes, your children will technically do what you demand in your presence, but when they are out of your sight, which is most of the time, they will quickly learn to lie and maintain a facade to keep the peace. Parents don't realize how little control they actually have over their children's lives and behaviors.

Life lessons that instill evasiveness can be more damaging to the children than striking them. I worked very hard to remove evasiveness and secrecy between me and my children. Of course my children did not tell me everything, and they should not. Everything they go through is my concern, but most if it is none of my business.

If you take my advice and portray a masculine nonjudgmental presence, you can teach empowering life lessons and grow closer to your child.

I usually start off saying something like this:

"My initial reaction to your request is that I think (insert behavior here) will be bad for you, or your motivations are not based on your needs. It is important to note that I know I am not always right and that I can only make suggestions based on my experience, which I know is different than yours.

I can see your urgency and excitement and can tell this can easily escalate if you don't get the answer you want. Let's back up here and remember how Dad communicates with you and how I have taught you that we need to discuss all things with love, respect, and with a mutual appreciation. You seem extremely desperate to have or do this thing. Let's talk about that desperation first, as you know I feel desperation is a bad thing for us to feel. Desperation can lead us to severely compromise ourselves."

When you see a child is desperate to follow the crowd at all costs, this is the time to have a much broader discussion about the dangers of peer pressure. Most of these urgent emotionally-charged "requests" are usually motivated by an acute anxiety of being an outcast, "uncool," and losing social status.

When my children were little, I created a teaching device called "The Desert Island Question." I find almost any child in grade school can understand it.

The Desert Island Question basically asks, "If you were on a desert island and would never see another person again and could never view yourself in a mirror, would you still feel the same urgency to do what you want to do?"

This question is meant to create a teaching moment. In my experience, with my three daughters, when socially pressured requests are asked of me, reframing their request with The Desert Island Question really puts things in proper perspective for them. Then a discussion can begin in which you are teaching your children, not just dictating to them.

My children started using The Desert Island Question in their minds very quickly from a young age. A seven-year-old can understand this, and that is when I started to use it as a parenting tool. This type of parenting makes your children independent thinkers and gives them real tools that they can use their entire lives.

The Desert Island Question is a simple method to teach a child self-observation.

Let's apply this to our pink hair example. Is it possible, on a desert island, that a thirteen-year-old may believe she needs pink hair just to feel whole, even though she can't see the pink hair? Sure. Might that require therapy that goes beyond the scope of this book? Highly likely.

When guided through the exercise, a child may see the outside influences guiding her actions. That is a breakthrough.

Above all else, I am a realist. I know my parenting strategies can sometimes have absolutely no affect at all, and your child may escalate emotionally and verbally. Your child may find a way to still do the behavior in question without your knowledge.

You can only control YOU, and that is what you must do. At all costs, do not be baited into a heightened emotional response.

**You must remain the masculine
nonjudgmental sanctuary.**

I assure you that if you follow my advice for communicating with your children starting now, you will grow ever closer to them, you will encounter much less friction, and, most importantly, your children will be much more mature than their peers at every stage of their development.

What is the main point? Let's go back to this chapter's title.

Desperation leads to self-compromise leads to enslavement.

The lesson in this chapter is something they will use for the rest of their lives and eventually share with their children.

When you are long gone, your Foxhole Fathering will be impacting your grandchildren and great-grandchildren.

BECOME A CALM PERSPECTIVE IN YOUR CHILD'S HEAD

Wouldn't it be great if you could have a conversation with your children even when you're not with them? Imagine your child, when confronted with a serious life problem, being able to use your thought process as another perspective besides their own to reference. It would be like having a conversation with you when you are not there.

This goes well beyond most fathers' goals for their parenting. Many fathers are happy if their children will listen to them just some of the time. Many parents are reactionary, and they simply want to defuse the current situation and make a child stop a certain behavior.

The Foxhole Father goes well beyond that. If you handle communication with your children the right way, your thought process and love will be with them constantly. They will learn to respect and appreciate your advice and perspectives. They will seek out your nonjudgmental father's advice, even when they are not with you.

By using the advice I've laid out in this book, your masculine nonjudgmental bond will strengthen and help your child grow in so many ways. This leads to them trusting your intentions, which leads to them trusting your thought processes.

When you have reached this level of bond with your children, they are always assuming your intentions are good for them. I cannot stress enough the importance of this concept. Strive to be this type of father by showing you always have their best interest at heart.

You can achieve this great level of parenting. You can have children who come to you when they have a problem. You can have children who want to refer to your perspective and advice in their heads when they come upon a life problem in your absence.

This is not to say they should listen to everything you advise. Quite the contrary, I have raised my daughters to realize I am not always right. Your children might be at a crossroads a hundred times each day. Your advice to them may be to go right and not left, for example. You have to humble yourself to the fact that your best thought process may not give the best answers for them. The best answer for them may be to turn left.

I taught my children that my thoughts and advice may not always give them the correct answers. That sounds very controversial to most parents, but I didn't want my children to believe they should blindly follow my orders. I wanted them to make their own decisions, including my advice in their thought process. I believe this fostered independent thought, a vital life skill for them to have.

I realize there are times, especially when children are very young, that "because I said so" is the end of the conversation. As they get older, though, this will work less and less, unless your children are scared of you.

How your children feel and how things impact them are the only things that matter. Our job as fathers is to expand their basic understanding of how their life choices and experience can impact them. As parents we have a life full of experiences and corresponding consequences that we can share with our children. You are the best resource of worldly knowledge for your children.

The Foxhole Father's failures and achievements become the basis for his children's greatest life lessons.

What do all parents want? To give their children any advantage they can. Your children can benefit from your life experience and avoid mistakes and pitfalls that hindered you growing up and as an adult.

Remember, your parenting goal is to filter everything through what is best for your children.

Unfortunately, some parents want to have the absolute control over every aspect of their children's lives. This is a dramatic mistake and a great fathering illusion.

If you believe you have absolute authority and control over your child's life, it is only because your child has learned to make sure you believe that.

You need to tell your children that they have to make the right decisions for themselves. Your thoughts about what is best for them is simply one perspective they should consider. This empowers them greatly.

If you establish the correct communication patterns with them, then not only will they come to you when they have a problem, they will also be better able to make the correct decisions for themselves.

As I said above, and as the title of this chapter states, you want to become a calm perspective in their head. I can describe it this way. My children can have a conversation with me even when I am not there. I have tried, not always successfully, to never give my children a reason to fear me or my reactions. What does this do? My children are not preoccupied with my reactions nor do they worry about my emotional state or my needs. They can live their lives openly and deliberately. They are unencumbered by my emotional system repressing them. All children deserve that. You can give this to your children as well.

Think of your experience with your parents.

- Were you raised to worry about our parents' reactions?
- Were you raised emotionally flinching in your home?
- Many of our parents were not a safe haven for us, emotionally or physically.

Many of us were not raised by Foxhole Fathers.

I have said it many times, and I will say it again. Your children should never have to worry about your emotional system. So often today, children are driven to certain behaviors by feelings of guilt or fear. This is a terrible lesson to teach your child.

So many children are forced to consider the emotional state of their parents. To me, this is a type of child abuse. Remember, you are your children's main example, and in the future they will be comfortable with the type of relationship you have established with them. So, if you're a dictatorial parent who rules by fear, intimidation, and guilt, that is exactly the type of romantic and personal relationships they will seek out.

No thoughtful parent would want this for his or her children. And the good news is that we can control it. We can have the greatest impact on the future happiness of our children. It all stems from how we act and how we treat them. The life lessons that you are consciously and subconsciously embedding in your children's minds and hearts will be with them until their dying day. No matter what you are doing, the impact on your children should be considered. This is even when they're not with you. How you live your life and the goals you choose will greatly impact your children.

You need to be a completely deliberate parent. Every time you interact with your children, or they observe your behavior, you are impacting their future decisions. It doesn't matter how long the interaction is, nor how intense. You could be helping with homework or simply going to the store together. Your children could hear a phone conversation you're having and that could influence them.

Many fathers put more time into their fantasy football league than they do their children. It is time to take an honest assessment of your fathering. And if you find you truly are not giving adequate attention and time to your children's development, then I urge you to make the necessary changes immediately to put your children first from now on.

Your children need their father much more than you may realize. Even if you are completely absent from their lives, you still are having a direct impact on their development and the types of masculine behaviors they will see as normal.

Changing the way we communicate with our children will give them a great advantage over other children. The amount of emotional and intellectual time that children expend worrying about what their parents think is something that can severely degrade a child's development.

What type of conversations, in their heads, do you want your children to have with you? When they are in bad place, worried or afraid, and you are not there with them, what thoughts about you do you want them to have at that moment? So many children have an added fear of their parents to deal with on top of bad situations.

For your children, those moments can be filled with thoughts of love, respect, peace, and nonjudgment. Your children can be soothed by your nonjudgmental masculine parenting, and this can make all the difference to them during any hard time.

Wouldn't that be great for your children? I think the answer is yes.

Starting right now, you can give it to them.

(BEFORE) FORGIVENESS

Hurt usually comes before forgiveness. The term "hurt" is overused today.

Learning how to forgive is an important life lesson for all of us.

I take a unique approach to forgiveness. My approach is an extension of my fathering philosophy, specifically how I filter others' actions.

Forgiveness is usually preceded by someone feeling hurt, and that "hurt" is the heart of this discussion.

So before I discuss teaching your children about forgiveness, let me show you how I handle disappointments in my relationships.

I call this (before) forgiveness.

I rarely have ever felt that someone in my life has hurt me. Yes, people have done many things I don't like, but I always assume they are doing the best that they can for me in those instances. If that is the case, then they did not hurt me.

I am not saying that things cannot upset me, or that I cannot feel disappointment when people do things I don't like.

Most times, when people are "hurt," they actually just didn't like something someone did or said. They would have loved that person to have done something else. Most people, in our lives, are going through their tough day and doing the best they can. It is impossible for everyone in your life to love you perfectly and satisfy all of your emotional and physical expectations. People don't have to do everything we want them to do.

Instead of allowing others to be human, some choose the negative route. Instead of trying to find innocent reasons why someone in their life didn't consider them fully, or did something that seems thoughtless, they will get deep into their self-pity and start accusing the other person of hurting them. This is a destructive way of handling things. The other person, who is innocent, is suddenly put on the defensive, and that is not justified. Bringing accusatory emotional outbursts into someone else's space should be avoided.

Being hurt, to me, needs to stem from someone intentionally doing something to slight me. So, if someone in my life is innocently going about his day and he simply does something I don't like, I cannot be hurt and he doesn't need to be forgiven at all.

People cannot be perfect. People cannot always love us in the way we would like.

Life is full of disappointments; that does not mean someone has done something wrong to you.

People would feel "hurt" much less often if they would self-observe and humanize people and situations.

This is an uncommon concept. But once I get people to understand it, it can really open them up to an even happier life. I have taught this to my children. Imagine if your children rarely felt hurt.

If someone innocently did something you don't like, they don't need to be forgiven for anything.

When you are hurt, you have voluntarily become the victim of someone else. This adds an unnecessary layer of drama to the relationship. It may postpone or even eliminate objective and loving discussions, which are required for the relationship to grow.

How many of us have relationships that are "stuck" in the quicksand of someone's hurt feelings?

Imagine if people in your life never told you that you hurt them? Imagine discussing what happens in relationships without the usual adversarial attitudes and confrontations?

If people accuse you of hurting them, never negate their feelings. Try to teach them the philosophy that is in this chapter. Their feeling hurt is much worse for them than it is for you. Discuss the idea that you always have good intentions for them and that you want all discussions to begin with that thought. Teach them that there is a way to handle these situations with much less stress and much more love and understanding.

You can have these healthy interactions and teach your children how to as well. If you do, your children will learn to not allow the actions of others to negatively impact their emotions, which is a great gift.

You, as their Foxhole Father, can embody this life lesson by removing all negative feelings you have with anyone in your life. We all know people who carry grudges and remain the victims of what other people have done. You will read throughout this book about how I have learned to never allow anything or anyone to impact my emotional system negatively. Are you feeling hurt by others very often? If so, take a step back and self-observe using the tools from this chapter.

What does this have to do with forgiveness?

Teach your children that it is best to move on from the transgressions of others and to never carry anger or hatred, especially when someone is doing the best they can.

You should try to get past the transgressions of others, even if they were intentional. You should not define yourself by another person or anything else outside of you. You can learn how to stop allowing things outside of you to impact you in negative ways.

Now, go back and reread that last paragraph, but this time reword it so you can teach your children the same lessons.

If someone intentionally slighted you, you may need to remove them from your life, leaving them in the past, without any lingering hurt or anger. You should be left with a lesson learned. Someone intentionally hurting you is not something to be taken lightly. Too many people, for wanting to keep the peace, turn a blind eye to this, only to become a victim over and over again.

From now on, when someone does something you don't like, self-observe and control where your emotional system takes you.

Instead of feeling hurt, angry, and abused, you can choose to discuss the problem, express why what happened was bad for you, and see if there is a way to continue that relationship in a positive way for both of you.

Was it innocent? Did the person have bad intentions? These are the most important questions to ask before you react.

Sometimes, things happen that are forgivable, but it may be necessary to end that relationship. Someone could have an innocent habit that is not acceptable to you. In that case, you need to be strong enough to walk away from that person. People may be good intentioned, but they may not meet your needs.

You can't change someone, and you can't change their expressions of love for you. You can't make someone love you the way you need.

Many people hold grudges for a lifetime. Think about this now in the context of what you have just read in this chapter. You should see this is unnecessary and unhealthy.

Back to forgiveness.

Teach your children to accept a sincere apology. People are human and will do things innocently that we don't like. This does not mean they are bad people or that you have a right to attack and abuse them.

Just as you have shown your children patience and love and understanding, your children need to be taught the benefits of extending these same traits but without compromising their own needs.

It is your job to teach them to not carry painful emotional baggage through their lives.

If you are someone who is carrying hurt feelings and grudges for a very long time, consider seeking professional help to free yourself from that emotional prison.

Feelings of hurt, anger, and being a victim of others serves no positive purpose for your life. Take back control of your emotional system. If you live your life eliminating these feelings, your children will learn this trait, and it will come naturally to them.

It would be a great gift for them.

Can you imagine children who handle relationship conflicts and disappointment this way? They may avoid so much unnecessary pain during their lives and experience so much more joy.

It all starts (before) forgiveness.

How does this help you to be a better father? These ideas that you just learned can help your kids' teen years be much more peaceful for you.

As children enter their teens and begin to speak in a more mature way, many parents can forget that they are still children. They have the ability to use adult language, sometimes against us, and it is easy for us to be drawn into emotionally painful exchanges with them. It is so easy to be "hurt" by our children if we are not careful.

When there were heated discussions with my kids and things turned personal, I paused and realized they were only children. Would I get emotionally hurt if a newborn was crying in her crib? Of course not.

During their teen years, children become more social, and your oversight of them can cause a tremendous amount of strain and anger. These times and situations can quickly become emotionally charged, and your child may lash out at you in anger with harsh words.

Although they are using adult language, don't ever get baited by their personal attacks. Let their words flow around you with no emotional impact, just as a crying baby would not cause you any emotional pain. If you learn to do this, your children may stop personally attacking you, as it will not have the desired effect.

When their outburst is done, always come back calmly to the topic at hand, ignoring whatever they said that was off topic, no matter how harsh it may have been. Sometimes loud outbursts are just your children's attempts at diverting your attention from what was causing the friction in the first place.

Don't ever let anything weaken your rules or stop you from demanding important information from your teen.

So many parents tell their children they are hurting them. When you do this, you are acting in an immature way, and this is bad for both of you.

I believe it is not possible for a non-adult child to hurt you, no matter what they do or say.

In the bigger Foxhole Father picture, your feelings do not matter anyway, right?

Try to eliminate "hurt" from your vocabulary, especially in interactions with your children. Doing this will get the focus back on your children's needs and away from yours, and that is where all father-child conversations should be centered.

NEVER DEMONIZE "NORMAL" BEHAVIOR

Children are exposed to much more normal "adult" behaviors than we can imagine, even at their earliest ages. You can only shelter your children from so much. Many parents want to shelter their children from too much of what is actually just "normal" life. Your job is to give them the coping mechanisms, perspective, and strength to interpret the "life" they will encounter now and forever.

If a behavior is a normal "adult" behavior, never demonize it to your child.

I am not condoning teenagers engaging in adult behaviors, just suggesting parenting methods to discuss them.

They are constantly exposed to adult behaviors, especially at home and in the media. It makes sense that they try to emulate those behaviors.

I learned that it is not possible to micromanage situations my children will encounter. I felt that if I empowered them with the right life tools, I didn't have to. With your help, your children will make decisions that are best for them, especially when you are not there.

When we see our kids engaging in a normal adult behavior (sex, drinking, etc.), we can get incredibly frightened and angry. We need to be extra vigilant and exercise self-control and never allow those base feelings to guide our parenting.

You want your children to talk to you. You want your children to tell you their deepest fears and concerns about what they are seeing in the world around them, especially about normal adult behaviors.

It is so easy for a child to become secretive if your demeanor during intense discussions is not controlled. I realize how hard it is to control your reactions when you are afraid for your child, but it imperative that you do.

Take an objective look at yourself. What examples are you setting? Make sure your personal actions strengthen, not weaken, your advice to your children.

If you demonize normal adult behaviors, some that they may see you doing, of course they may see you as a hypocrite and ignore you.

A common mistake: Dad, his third beer of the night in his hand, tells his son to not drink at his friend's party. This is completely confusing and ridiculous to his son.

Example of a teenager engaging in a normal adult behavior:

Your thirteen-year-old son comes home from a party and tells you there was a lot drinking. Some of the kids drank so much they got sick and had to be taken to the hospital in an ambulance. He admits to having had one beer. He is visibly shaken by this new experience.

Many parents, me included, could have many intense reactions to this.

It is at these moments when parents make critical mistakes in communication, especially when it relates to a normal adult behavior.

They may allow intense personal feelings to control the discussion. They may start what I call "The Interrogation." They may ask:

- Which kids brought the alcohol?
- Who was drunk?
- Did the parents know?
- Where were the parents during this?
- They may scream, "You are never going to that house ever again!"

Notice there was not one question about how the child felt about it.

Once this "interrogation" starts, it is very hard to get back to a positive parenting role. Your child will feel extremely pressured. Your child has done nothing wrong, and he should be treated accordingly. Many parents put their children on the defensive almost immediately when discussing sensitive topics. This is a costly parenting mistake, and valuable life lessons could be lost.

You can't guide your child without taking the time to listen to him. He has seen or heard something that is foreign to him. He is confused and frightened. In these situations, it is always best to allow your child to express himself completely. If you do this, you will be able to lovingly address all of his concerns when he needs it most, right now.

Remember, this may be the first drunken episode he has ever witnessed. Give it the gravity and importance it deserves.

Each child can have the same experience, but he or she will need to be parented in different ways. As always, your parenting does not start with your feelings. Your feelings do not matter. Your child's needs are all that matter, and your job is to help him or her navigate this new and troubling situation. Imagine that you had identical triplets coming to you at the same time. Your parenting should be different for each one, based on their individual needs.

If the behavior in question could eventually become a normal behavior for your child, tell him that, but explain the physical and emotional context where it is appropriate. In this case, drinking alcohol is a normal adult behavior, but drinking until you are impaired is not—ever.

Prepare your children for these situations well ahead of time, while they are young. Teach them that feeling the effects of alcohol, even on a small level, can be incredibly dangerous. Explain why.

Long before they were exposed to alcohol socially, I taught my kids how to protect themselves from its danger.

There may be times when your children feel they are old enough to act in certain ways, sexually or otherwise. All you can do is explain how the behaviors can harm them and how to protect themselves. You should discuss that they may not have the emotional maturity for certain activities.

Explain why, calmly, the behavior may impact their lives in a negative way. Tell your children that drinking can lead to falling because their balance can be off. Remind your daughters that when they are impaired, they are at risk of being taken advantage of by male predators.

These are teaching moments and a time for personal growth and understanding for both you and your child.

If you prepare your child, through nonjudgmental communication, there is a greater chance your child will not blindly follow the crowd. This will lead to your children taking much fewer risks with their safety.

When your children decide to engage in an adult behavior, you will at least know it is based on their internal desire and personal decision only, and not social pressure.

Again, we cannot micromanage our children's lives, and they will do things we disagree with. Getting them to a point of truly independent decision making based on what they feel is right for them is the parenting success we are looking for.

If you don't overreact to their life's questions about normal adult behaviors, you will create mature, thoughtful, and successful children.

Most importantly, you will create children who will continually seek out your guidance, especially when they are troubled. That is the greatest success you can achieve as a parent.

Your adult behaviors will be seen as the most normal to your children. Be extremely mindful of this.

Are you telling your children to not engage in behaviors they see you doing? No matter what you say to them, your behavior will condone the same behavior in them.

Don't be shocked when they follow your example.

ALWAYS BE ON YOUR CHILDREN'S SIDE

The Foxhole Father is his children's advocate and protector. He is never their adversary.

The Foxhole Father is the expert on his children and knows them best.

For example, if they get into trouble in school, it is easy for them to see you as another adult who is against them and is judging them. This is all too common, and you need to be very conscious of your reactions and interactions with your child in these situations. First, tell your child that you are not assuming that any allegations are true. In fact, you may disagree with what school personnel have charged them with. This happened to me many times. I have an entire chapter dedicated to interacting with educators. I learned to never automatically assume that a teacher, guidance counselor, or principal was right to bring a disciplinary action against my child. I also learned to question teachers about grades that didn't seem to make sense.

Once you understand all of the facts, discuss what happened in a nonjudgmental way. Please be mindful that teenagers may feel very isolated already, and if their parents are harsh and judgmental and seem to be taking the side of the school, it can make them retract even further. Avoiding further retraction should be on your mind.

If you are brought in for a conference and your child is of an appropriate age, make sure he accompanies you. Avoid being defensive in the meeting, and make sure your child sees you as his or her advocate. This never means defending your child when it is apparent that rules were broken. You may agree completely with what the school personnel are saying and that your child's behavior has no place in school. If you agree that disciplinary actions need to be taken, then say so. There should always be consequences when rules are broken.

When representing his child, the Foxhole Father is diplomatic, calculating, and unemotional, and he negotiates the best outcomes for his child.

After such a meeting, the two of you can discuss how you handled the situation on his behalf. Always look for feedback about your parenting from your children, especially in situations such as this. If you handle things the right way, your child will see you as his advocate—someone who is trying to negotiate the best possible outcome for him.

You should also refer back to my basic Foxhole Father philosophy, and clearly explain how this situation could negatively impact your child in the long run. As always, never use words of judgments or loud tones.

Privacy and Respect

Your children should expect a certain amount of privacy and respect, even during times of tension between you.

Especially in public, your children should expect your discretion in conversations, especially when you are discussing their behavior or something personal.

We all have seen parents loudly reprimanding their children. This should never happen. There may be times when you physically have to stop a child's behavior. This does not mean striking them, but restraining them to force the behavior to stop.

You want people outside your family to see you as your child's supportive and strong advocate—other parents, teachers, bosses, friends, etc. You and your children are on the same side, and they should always feel completely insulated, even when there is friction or drama.

The Foxhole Father never judges his child or injects his personal feelings into situations.

Your children should always know you are on their side, acting in their best interest and teaching them how their actions may impact their lives negatively.

The world should always see you as your children's advocate and protector.

Most situations are temporary, but your Foxhole Fathering lessons are embedded forever. Your Foxhole Father parenting moments will help them throughout their lives, especially when you are not there immediately to help them with something. They will be able to use the Foxhole Fathering perspective you have nurtured in their hearts and minds, and get advice from you even when you are not there.

TEENAGERS ARE JUST LIKE NEWBORNS

This chapter is filled with advice I wish I had received when my first child became a teenager.

When the teenage years start, I want you to imagine that the calendar has been reset and your teenager is a brand new baby again.

Remember when your first child was born? Many of us had no idea what to truly expect. I read many books ahead of time, and although they were slightly helpful, nothing could prepare me for what it was like to take care of a child in real time and three dimensions.

I can compare it to my experience scuba diving. Before my first real dive, I had read many diving books. Some were technical and included things like schematics of equipment and an explanation of what diving at depth does to your body. Some were filled with personal diving adventure stories.

The diving books and classes were all very enjoyable and informative, but they could not prepare me for my first deep dive with sharks at 150 feet.

I have heard similar feelings from soldiers I have met. Boots on the ground in enemy territory is when real training and understanding begins.

The same holds true for a newborn baby. My first true moment of parenting reality happened when my firstborn was strapped in the car seat as we left the hospital. The car doors were shut. Then we watched the nurse walk away from us pushing the wheelchair my daughter's mother had just gotten out of. The hospital entrance doors swooshed open, the nurse walked through them, and then swoosh, the doors closed and I was officially a father. I looked behind me at the car seat, and for the first time, I felt responsible for the life of someone else. It took my breath away. I had never felt such fear. I clutched the steering wheel as tightly as

I could to try to stop my arms and hands from trembling.

So, I learned as I went from moment to moment. A newborn is completely helpless, and my job was to take care of her needs, putting my personal needs on the back burner. Newborns cry when they are uncomfortable for any reason, and I learned quickly what each of her cries meant.

I want you to go back to those earliest moments of having a newborn baby at home. There was never a time where you took it personally that the baby was crying, even in the middle of the night, correct? I want you to apply the same mindset to your teenager.

In the first few years of life, your child goes through so many developmental milestones: walking, talking, potty training, learning social skills. During all of these you were focused on your child's needs and development, ignoring your needs and not taking it personally when your child had a tantrum or disobeyed you.

So much development happens in the first four years of a child's life. A baby is truly helpless and reliant on you to be selfless, nurturing, patient, and helpful.

When they become teenagers, a similar process happens again. There will be a few years when there are many developmental milestones. These will be new for both of you, just as walking, talking, and potty training were. There is an exponential amount of growth for your child during this time on so many emotional and biological levels.

Even though they seem like young adults, I want you to approach having a teenager the same way you approached your newborn.

Raising a teenager is an unknown world for us, yet most parents don't realize this. It is truly as if your child has been reborn again. So, you are technically a brand new father again.

Like a newborn, teenagers are truly helpless and discovering new parts of the world. They are reliant on you to be selfless, nurturing, patient, and helpful.

Fathers should regroup and understand that this is totally unknown territory. If you do this, it can truly help to smooth out the teenage years.

How so?

A fourteen-year-old yelling that he doesn't want to do his homework is no different than a hungry baby crying in a crib. You didn't take it personally when a baby was crying and screaming at you, so avoid that now.

It was sometimes very hard for me, but I tried to never let my teenagers' aggressive behavior or yelling impact me, especially in front of them. The more upset I got, the less focus I put on parenting my child. That is never good.

I also realized that loud outbursts from teenagers, sometimes including harsh words directed at me, were mostly a smoke screen and just a way for the teenager to distract me from the real topic at hand.

Teenagers, unlike babies, can use adult words, and those can hurt us and they know it. This is where self-observation and self-control come in. Be prepared for such things. Don't allow yourself to be emotionally immersed in these types of exchanges with your teenager.

Visualize yourself as a piece of granite in the middle of a raging river. The rushing water (your child's harsh words) flow around you, unable to permeate you.

I learned to stay calm and not let things get to me. I treated my teenagers like children who simply needed me to be the parent and nurture them through whatever they were going through.

Especially during the teenage years, being the masculine nonjudgmental sanctuary is extremely important. This means being strong enough to ignore the hurt that may be caused from arguments with your teenager and staying focused on filtering all of your actions through what is best for them—just like you did when they were infants.

If you are prepared and have this mindset, parenting a teenager can be much easier for you emotionally. You both will benefit if you do this.

There are more life stages your children will go through when having this newborn mentality can really help you be a better father: When they go off to college, graduate from college and get a first job, get married, become a parent.

Teenagers are just like newborns. Having that mindset may help make a greater success of your children's teenage years.

SCHOOL/ACTIVITIES –
YOU ARE THE MAIN EDUCATOR OF YOUR CHILDREN

If you haven't already done so, please read the section in Quick Action Guide, "Kids' Grades and Extracurricular Activities," page 37 before continuing with this section.

In my experience of raising three children, I discovered many instances in which teachers and other school employees acted as if they didn't have to answer to me. I had to correct them many times.

It is important that you establish your presence clearly and early with all of the school personnel who will interact with your children. There are some men, myself included at first, who feel insecure in the school environment. I am not sure why we sometimes feel that way, but please self-observe and correct those feelings.

You must maintain direct daily oversight of your child's education, both in school and at home.

At the start of each new school year, I do the following:

1. Get all teachers emails and work phone numbers with extensions.
2. Send test emails to each and request acknowledgements.
3. Make an introductory phone call to all teachers/instructors/coaches.
4. Attend all children's school functions, especially back-to-school night.
5. Make sure I am entered in the school database as an equal parent who will receive all correspondence, including phone calls, that relate to my children.

This goes for married and coupled Foxhole Fathers as well single ones. Make sure your presence and goals for your children are known to everyone who interacts with your children. It is not just the responsibility of your children's mother.

Quite often it is the mother who takes care of school-related responsibilities. You need to be proactive here and make sure your voice and influence are heard as well.

I believe my children benefited greatly by knowing that I was just as interested and available for their academic needs as their mother.

It is imperative that you establish clear channels of communication with your children's teachers, guidance counselor, and educational administrative staff (principal, vice principal, etc.).

Most teachers see your children less than one hour per day. In all situations, you know what is best for them. Over the past few decades, unfortunately, teachers have needed to take on a personal mentoring role with some children. Some parents are absent. I believe there is a place for teachers to fill in those gaps, but with your children it remains with you only.

Teaching social and life skills are the parents' responsibility. A teacher's main focus should be maximizing your children's academic achievement. Feedback from teachers is a valuable resource regarding your children's behavior and academic progress. Take advantage of this and demand it.

Most schools have an online system where parents can check daily progress. Find out if your children's school has this. If so, obtain login/user credentials from the school right away. Even though an online system may be in place, you should request additional information on a regular basis from the teachers. For example, if your child is not performing, the teachers should be communicating this with you immediately.

If your school does not have an online system, or if the online system does not provide you with enough detailed information, request a paper progress report from each teacher every Friday. Make sure you receive the accumulated letter grade and numeric grade. I personally did this during most of my children's high school years, as there was no online system.

You should approach educators with respect, but also with specific and targeted requests and expectations. The teachers work for you and your children, and you should let it be known that you have final oversight and say regarding your children's education.

The Foxhole Father is the expert on his children and, along with his children's mother, is their main educator.

I have a frank discussion with all parties to ensure the parents, my child, and the teacher are all responsible for making sure my child performs to the best of her ability in the classroom. I guarantee that my children and I will give 100% effort, and I ask the teachers to guarantee the same.

One of the most important benefits you will derive from this approach is that the teachers will know you are actively monitoring their performance as well as your children's.

The Foxhole Father has strict oversight of anyone interacting with his children.

WHAT DO YOU THINK?

I ask this of my children when they come to me with a question or problem:

"It doesn't matter what I think, what do you think?"

This helped my children gain confidence in using their own decision-making tools.

Before I offer my opinions or advice, I want my children to first use their own critical thinking and emotional skills when they have a problem or need direction. Then, after they share their feelings and thought process with me, I help them further analyze things, always molding my discussions based on what is best for them.

What does your child think about situations? OUR filters, or our initial gut reactions, may not lead to what is best for them.

Remember the main theme of this book is, "What is best for my children?"

If you take your personal emotional filters out of the decision-making process, and OBJECTIVELY make decisions for your children based solely on their best interest and needs, 99% of the time you will be making the best possible decision for them.

A good example:

It is time for high school football tryouts. Your youngest son has been playing tackle football since he was ten years old. He excels at this. In your mind your sons must play football. Period. All of your sons know you feel this way. You played college football and almost went pro. Now at fourteen, your son is entering high school in the fall. Your two eldest sons got athletic scholarships and are playing college football now as you did. Your youngest shows even more potential than your two eldest sons did. Your two eldest love the game, but your youngest son hates the game. You have no idea that he feels that way. Did you ever ask him? What does he think?

Your youngest approaches you and shows the courage to tell you he does not want to play football. At these moments you will feel so many emotions. Most of them will be based on what you want or what you feel is right, without fully considering what is best for your son.

As a Foxhole Father, you should pause and ask your son to take his time explaining his feelings. If you are feeling fear or anger or worry, you should not show this at all.

Once your son is through explaining himself, discuss all the potential negative and positive consequences you can see with his decision that he may not.

In this case, his athletic talent may provide him with scholarships for college and may give him access to colleges he may not otherwise have. This should be part of his decision-making process.

Ultimately, you have to decide if you are going to try to force him to play football against his will if he does not want to play. You may have to if you truly believe it is in his best interest to do so.

What is best for him? If you ignore your personal feelings, then the answer becomes easier to see. He may choose to continue playing as part of his college planning.

It should not matter to your son that you have personal reasons for wanting him to play football, and you should tell him that.

Instilling a sense of self and teaching children that their affirmations should only come from within is at the core of Foxhole Fatherhood.

I have taught my children that it does not matter what I think about them at all. If I glorify them, it should have no bearing on their self-image or self-esteem. And conversely, and most importantly, if I don't approve of what they are doing, that should also have no bearing on their self-image or self-esteem. Even with this mindset, I know that it is natural for my children to sometimes seek my approval and care about my opinions.

When my children's friends' parents hear that I believe my personal feelings are less important than my children's, they are flabbergasted. Some parents seem to want to exercise control over their children's thoughts and actions. This can become emotional extortion or coercion. Various ploys using guilt, fear of loss, fear of punishment, fear of abuse, etc. are used to control a child's behavior. Many parental tactics manipulate a child's self-worth to control his or her behavior.

These manipulative methods can scar children for life. Just as a father who physically abuses a child teaches a terrible lesson, a parent who uses aggressive and controlling parenting methods does the same. Unfortunately, these learned abusive tools may surface in their future relationships. The cycle is constantly continued.

So, what does this have to do with the topic of this chapter? Everything.

You have a choice to change the parenting dynamics inside of you. You can learn to self-observe and completely rewrite the book on the father you will be from now on.

The Foxhole Father builds a fathering relationship with his children from scratch, based on what is best for them.

When confronted with a behavioral issue or other situation from your children, give them all the time they need to express what they think and feel. If this step is skipped, there is no way of knowing how to father them through the problem.

The situation alone does not provide enough information. If necessary, ask them to discuss their urgency and their fears. Ask them what would happen if they didn't engage in a certain behavior? Would there be a backlash? Would they lose social support? If you see peer pressure playing a role, discuss how that pressure needs to be ignored and how it should be unacceptable to them. Open up a discussion about how allowing external influences to guide our decisions is relinquishing our most important power over our lives, self-rule.

When they have finished, explain all of your concerns as they relate to them. Give them advice based on your life's experience, sharing similar problems you have had to work through.

Of course there are parenting decisions based on justified parental fears when the child's feelings cannot be considered.

Ask your children to mirror back your concerns and advice so you are sure they heard you clearly. Make sure they always know that you only care about their best interest. It is all out of loving them, not controlling them. That is the message.

A point here about communication. Regardless of the topic, communications of all kinds must be respectful in your space and your home. You and your children deserve this. This teaches a vital lesson, which I want my children to demand in their space. I want them to see this as normal. Remember, life events and issues are all temporary, but how you communicate with your children should be consistent.

My children see loud and aggressive communication as completely unacceptable. I am very proud of that, and this is only because my home rarely included it. You can provide the same environment.

The Foxhole Father establishes guidelines for behavior and personal space that are healthy for his children at two years old and a hundred years old.

More important than the specific discussion you may be having is the emotional and physical environment in which you are having those discussions. Remember, your children may adopt your example as normal for the rest of their lives. Be sure to project healthy communication methods, so they will demand them from others the rest of their lives.

The basic advice in this chapter:

Ask, "What do you think?"
Sit back and listen.

If you implement the strategies in this book, your children will be much more willing to tell you.

122

TURN FRICTION AND DRAMA INTO
TEACHING MOMENTS

How can we turn friction and drama into teaching moments?

A situation with my daughter once occurred when I had asked her to do something for me for several days. On the fifth morning we were all in the kitchen, my three girls and me, and I brought this request up to my daughter again. She acted extremely annoyed, told me that what I had asked did not make any sense to her, and left the kitchen.

My other two daughters questioned how I was handling the situation, and they also questioned the validity and importance of my request.

The daughter with whom I was having a conflict was now out of the room, and instead of chasing her, I took this time with my other two daughters to turn that friction into a teaching moment.

The teaching moment had nothing to do with what my specific request had been with my other daughter.

What had really happened that was unacceptable to me? It went beyond a simple disagreement. My daughter was basically saying that my need should not be important to me, and it did not make sense. This was a subtle way of saying I was crazy and I was not thinking straight.

I told my other daughters that people have no right to make these judgments. We should never attempt to minimize the intensity of someone else's need or to question its importance. Many people don't always understand me, for example. Just because someone doesn't understand my thoughts doesn't mean those thoughts are not worthwhile. People just need to take the time to gain a deeper understanding through discussion.

We discussed how priorities are personal. They are subjective and relative, and others have no right to evaluate and judge them. I took a lot of time to discuss this, because I was trying to teach them about a behavior that should be considered unacceptable to them. As always, that is the Foxhole Fathering goal, to give your children tools to navigate life and relationships.

Our kitchen talk continued. I role-played situations in which people may deem their needs irrational and ignore them. I was able to get them to realize that for them, this would be unacceptable. Although the initial friction had been against me, my feelings were not part of the discussion.

As in all situations, I was ignoring what may have been a personal violation or neglect against me and was teaching them what I wanted them to demand and expect for themselves.

Some parents would have lost the teaching moment. They may have chased that other daughter out of the room, and things could have escalated.

Imagine that scenario. Your two other daughters, alone in the kitchen, listening to you have a yelling match with their sister. That should never happen. Instead, let the tension die down and use that time for teaching your other children valuable life lessons.

Friction can include yelling and hurtful words from your children. A baby screaming in a crib cannot hurt your feelings, though, correct? A teenager, although he or she can say hurtful things, is no different than the infant in a crib. Teenagers are children who need parents to guide them. I know you may feel incredibly hurt when angry words have been showered on you. That is a completely normal and human reaction. I raised three children, all adults now, and believe me, harsh words from them at five or fifteen could instantly break my heart. But I tried to ignore those personal feelings and stay focused on taking care of them. Try not to allow your teenagers' tantrums to impact your parenting.

You will see throughout this book that your feelings do not matter. Along that line, no matter what your children may say or scream at you, let it flow around you. It is hard to do this, but it will be one of the best parenting skills you will ever learn. The benefits to your children will be exponential. Many times children want to get you emotionally upset, as that will distract you from the topic at hand.

Imagine that you are a piece of granite with a raging river surrounding you. Never does the water permeate the granite; it simply flows around it.

In any interaction with my children, I place more importance on

HOW we interact than on the topic at hand. Friction and drama are all temporary.

In my home, I tried to establish what I call "respectful listening." The basic ground rules of respectful listening are:

1. You should not be interrupted until you are finished speaking.
2. Establish and keep direct eye contact.
3. There is no yelling in our house
4. The discussion stays on topic.
5. There are no mean words or personal attacks.
6. You may disagree on something, but that should not change the love you feel for each other.
7. It is not important that someone agrees with you.
8. If someone does something you don't like, assume they are doing the best they can, and it was not done on purpose.

Volatile topics will come up often. They are temporary, and then they are gone. The method of communication can be permanent, though. So make sure the communication is always done in a respectful, objective, and loving way every time.

Many times when I saw an interaction between my children escalating to a negative place, I would call a time-out and suggest there was a better way to communicate, regardless of what the topic was. The topic was none of my business. It was between them. But my fathering goal here was to make calm, respectful, and objective conversation the norm for them—to turn the friction and drama into teaching moments.

So, after I said my piece and had them agreeing with me about my communication methods, I would leave the room and let them discuss their personal issues alone, as it should be. There were times when they came to me to ask my opinion. It was at those the moments when I felt that my masculine nonjudgmental parenting style was working.

I wanted them to recoil from anyone who communicates with them aggressively, and now, as adults, they do.

I stopped many a nasty argument in its tracks this way. I did not take a side, and I didn't discuss the topic they were arguing about. Again, volatile topics will come and go constantly in our lives. I learned a long time ago that I cannot micromanage my kids' lives or problems.

I wanted to give them lessons in self-observation from the youngest age. I wanted them to be able to control their emotions and their demeanor, unlike so many other people who are out of control. I wanted to give them boundaries that they will use the rest of their lives when anyone is communicating with them.

This is a valuable life lesson you can pass along to your children as well.

In my home, the following were never allowed:

- Screaming
- Demeaning language
- Gossip
- Personal verbal attacks

I did this not to restrict my children, but to make these types of behaviors odd and foreign to them, especially from a man.

Moments of friction and drama can become teaching moments. You can use them to impart healthy social and communication skills, and to teach your children to use those skills and demand them from others.

They will thank you for this many years from now. Mine do.

BOYS AND GIRLS INTERACTING

I tried to never allow gender to play a role in my children's friend choices. So many parents seem to let puberty put a stop to their children having friends of a different gender. I think this is a mistake. This is not to say that there aren't special considerations when your child has a friend of the opposite gender.

As I am always thinking of their development and the people that I want them to become, I had to fight my irrational and socialized fear of my daughters being friends with boys after the onset of puberty.

My fear was palpable, and this came partly from my religious upbringing. I did not want them to learn what I had learned, that boys and girls cannot be platonic friends, and that after a certain age, friends of different genders will definitely become lovers.

Please hear this. Your sons and daughters are interacting with the opposite sex constantly. Texting, video chat, social networking, in the cafeteria, in the school parking lot, and on the bus.

You cannot micromanage those interactions, so focus on teaching your children to be responsible for themselves wherever they go.

I took every situation individually. Often times I expressed to my kids what my initial reactions were and discussed how they would have led me to bad parenting decisions. I discussed my initial knee-jerk feelings very often with my children and in many different situations, and it truly helped to humanize me to them.

Now, I still firmly believe in not inserting your emotional needs in your parenting, and when I discussed my thought processes with my children, I definitely was not doing that.

When I discussed my thought process about different situations, this was meant to teach them how to objectively analyze themselves in the future the same way. These were great examples of me self-observing. As

I have mentioned often in this book, always question your belief systems as well.

Imagine what a child learns when you approach parenting in the way I describe. Your child will learn and live this same approach in their lives, and that is exactly what your goal is. Most importantly, they will learn to expect to be treated in the same manner by other people, no matter the type of relationships they are in.

Always remember, you are their example of "normal."

Long before you realize it, your children will be in a position to have sex, do drugs, and consume alcohol. It is impossible for any parent to micromanage every situation. Your children are exposed to intense and dangerous social situations very often.

You will often hear many parents of daughters say things like, "You can't go to that party; there are boys there, and I don't trust them." Or "You can't go to the bowling alley with your friends after school; there are boys there that I don't know, and I don't trust them."

These types of things are said all the time because parents aren't thinking. Let's back up and look at those statements and dissect them a bit.

Are you afraid that your daughter is going to be sexually assaulted? If so, don't allow her to go to that place. If not, then you are really telling your daughter that you believe SHE is going to engage in behavior you disapprove of. To place some kind of blame ahead of time on boys you don't know is ridiculous and counterproductive.

Your daughter has a free will and is in total control of her behavior around boys. A parent should never place the blame for their children's behavior on others. In this case, we are preemptively doing that, right?

What message does this send to your daughter? Do you really want her to have a blanket distrust of boys to the point where she feels she can be sexually assaulted at any moment doing normal activities with friends? Or are you telling her that a normal behavior, being sexual or bowling, is something to fear? Are you teaching her that all boys are predators?

What other message can be read into such statements? None.

This is an example of regressive parenting, when a child is not taught anything useful, is left confused and bewildered, and is less likely to share her life with you. The next time she may lie about where she is going.

These types of comments about not trusting boys stems from an irrational parental fear and desire to protect our children. I understand it is from a loving place, but as I have tried to describe in this book, our initial knee-jerk emotional reactions can be the most damaging to our children's development.

Do you really have the fear that your daughter will engage in dangerous behavior? Then you need to discuss this with her. Do you feel she is not ready to be immersed in certain mixed social settings with no parental supervision? Then you need to discuss this with her. What are the real dangers for her?

Again, your daughter only has control over herself, and unless you feel there is a chance she will be physically attacked and forced to do things against her will, the conversation should focus on her needs, feelings, and level of maturity.

You have to self-observe and filter your reactions based on what is best for your child. That means being objective and realizing that acting on your gut fears may provide your child with the wrong life lesson.

The type of knee-jerk parenting in my bowling alley example can surface in us at any time. Teenagers are always approaching us with requests to do new things, and that can overwhelm us. It definitely overwhelmed me very often, especially because my children were with me every Friday and Saturday night after my divorce. My mind suddenly filled with images of my child out in an unknown and uncontrolled situation. My initial feeling often was to say, "No! You can't go there! Stay home! It is much safer here at home with me!"

Most times I was able to pause, take a breath, and have my daughters give me more information. The majority of the time they were allowed to go to the new place, and they had a great time.

Whenever I filtered my fathering through what was best for them, I always made the right decision.

The more you focus on becoming a Foxhole Father, the better the teen years will be for everyone.

ARE YOUR NEEDS BEING MET?

I want to restate an important point. If your children are discussing a topic or engaging in a behavior that is normal for adults to discuss or engage in, do not sensationalize or overreact while discussing these things with your children.

Sex, alcohol, drug use, impolite language—these are some of the things I am talking about. I do not condone any of these behaviors for teenagers. I am trying to share the Foxhole Father methodology for parenting your children through these situations.

These topics elicit very strong emotions in parents, one of them being fear. This fear can lead to destructive parenting and the loss of valuable life lessons during important moments in your child's development.

Example: Your twelve-year-old comes to you one day after school. She has a concerned and reflective look on her face.

She says, "Dad, there's a lot of kissing happening in school, and ... uh ... I kissed Billy McCarthy at lunch."

OK, STOP and breathe.

Some dads would portray an anxious/overbearing/judgmental/accusatory attitude at this time. Many times it is hard to stop your feelings from getting the better of you, and your communication can be filtered through your fears and other emotions.

Remember, The Foxhole Father ignores his personal feelings and focuses only on what is best for his child.

So, pause and breathe. Self-observe and control your reaction.

When I was presented with this discussion, I lightened the mood by saying, "Yeah, I remember. For me it was a Friday, pizza day at school. One moment I was taking a sip of my chocolate milk, and the next moment Susie Johnson tried to take advantage of me right there in the cafeteria."

These RARE conversations are the time that you need to be the most calm, understanding, and nonjudgmental. Your child has come to you with a concern. She needs guidance and is really asking for help understanding this new part of her world she has encountered. She is really discussing sex openly with you, although the topic is simply kissing.

Remember, if your child is comfortable enough to discuss sensitive topics with you, that is fantastic. It shows that you have been fathering the correct way. At these moments, be proud of what you have given your child. Many children would never discuss sensitive and personal topics with their parents.

How does a Foxhole Father handle these sensitive discussions? He always asks what his child feels first. Let her explain exactly why she has brought this up. As parents we have a tendency to assume the worst, and this evokes tremendous fear in us. You cannot let this fear be shown to your child. This will only make her draw back from you and feel that she has done something wrong! Let your child speak.

What you are trying to understand is your daughter's underlying reasons for kissing Billy McCarthy. Were her needs being met? This may sound odd when discussing a kiss between two twelve-year-olds in the lunchroom, but it is very significant.

After she has explained her concerns, feelings, and the impact this may have had on her, you must first let her know this behavior is a normal part of a mature, romantic relationship based on love. Do not demonize any behavior that will eventually be a normal part of her life. Kissing is a very normal part of adult relationships.

Now, if she wants to go skydiving or base jumping, something extremely dangerous, then of course you want to impart, with some emotion, that you feel those are very bad ideas.

This discussion about kissing in school can open up a great opportunity to discuss romantic needs and how significant it is for your child to have her needs met in ALL relationships.

Suppose your child elaborates that many classmates are kissing right in the hallway between classes. I would tell her that we should not judge her classmates and that behavior does not necessarily say anything about character or morals. Many people equate behaviors with a person's character or morality. This is a grave mistake.

I took these conversations as an opportunity to express to my children that is OK to want their needs to be met in all relationships, especially romantic ones. To see if your needs are being met, the first place to look is your underlying intentions and emotional reasons for doing something. To paraphrase a well-known proverb:

**Behaviors speaks louder than words,
but intentions speak louder than behaviors.**

For example:

Two girls in seventh grade are kissing boys in the hallway between classes.

The first girl is doing it out of fear that she will lose her boyfriend if she does not.

The second girl is doing so because she really wants to do it, she enjoys it, and she really wants to share that level of intimacy with her boyfriend. No pressure, no coercion, nothing fear-based.

So, we have identical behaviors, but the second girl is having her needs met, while the first girl is only kissing for fear of losing her boyfriend.

The intentions and emotional basis of the girls' behaviors are very different.

The age here is an important consideration of course. Can a twelve-year-old have the emotional depth to feel the romantic intimacy required to be physical at all at her age? Of course not. I definitely expressed this feeling to my teenagers. But I am a realist. A twelve-year-old, possibly in the onset of puberty, may believe she is ready to act like a grown woman. And I knew I could not stop her from engaging in most behaviors.

The Foxhole Father considers where his children are emotionally, physically, and psychologically in their development.

Age does not dictate maturity. Two sixteen-year-old boys, in the same situation, could need completely different parenting.

Back to the discussion with your daughter who has kissed a boy. In this case, you are having a sexual conversation with her. You need to think "big picture" here. Let's imagine she was thirty years old and came to you with a relationship question involving sex. Your response should always start with the same questions.

"How do you feel about this?"

"Are your needs being met?"

Your reactions may dictate how your children will feel about themselves with regard to these topics for the rest of their lives. You don't get many of these opportunities, so you must focus on your child and not your knee-jerk reactions.

If your reactions to sexual conversations reflect fear and anger, those feelings can be transferred to your child.

Let your kids know it is normal to think about and question anything in their lives, including drugs, sex, religion, relationships, school—and even you.

It is normal for them to have questions, to be scared, etc., and they should know that YOU are there unconditionally to help answer those questions in a safe and nonjudgmental way.

I have taught my daughters that you can love someone—a friend, boyfriend, etc.—but if your needs are not met, you need to remove them from your life. Don't fight it, and don't be angry that they do not meet your needs. They are not required to! People we are in relationships with need to be respected just as we need to be. The mature person will evaluate whether their needs are being met and, if not, will walk away.

Teach your children to never say things like, "If you loved me, you would do this or that." That is a form of bullying.

The Foxhole Father teaches his children that they cannot change someone and should never desire to.

Your children should be taught to expect that their needs are considered in all interactions that concern them in all relationships. This needs to be instilled from a young age. This does not mean they are catered to. It does mean within any kind of relationship, in matters that involve them emotionally or physically, their needs should be part of the decision-making process by the other party.

I will give an example.

Your nineteen-year-old son is dating a woman of the same age. For the most part they get along very well and seem to enjoy many of the same things: food, entertainment, spirituality. But when your son has something he wants to discuss about the relationship, she gets angry and defensive and says he is attacking her. She avoids him until he stops talking about it. He is left emotionally neglected, and that is never OK in any personal relationship. A significant need of your son is not being met. I would tell your son that it is not possible to change someone and that he should never try to. He needs to accept that his needs cannot be met by this person and peacefully walk away, no matter how hard it is. Tell him that of course he loves her, but that does not mean he must stay in an unfulfilling and painful relationship.

I want to emphasize my key thoughts on the topic of this chapter.

You can truly love someone, romantically or otherwise, but if they are not good for you and your needs are not being met, you can remove that person from your life without guilt.

Many girls learn to be extremely accommodating, especially with regard to romance. They may feel satisfied in knowing that the other person's needs are being met without considering theirs. Both boys and girls need to be taught that this is not enough.

You need to make sure they are conscious of their needs being met in all relationships and in all situations. Teach them that if their needs are not being met, a relationship CANNOT be fulfilling for them. They need to be strong enough to walk away from someone they deeply care about but who does not meet their needs.

Teach them that they deserve a friend, romantic partner, boss, etc. who will consider their needs as well as their own at all times.

With regards to their romantic needs being met, at the appropriate times I have taught my children that:

- Physically romantic behaviors should be preceded by an adult-level romantic love having developed between two people.
- As a teenager, the level of true romantic love needed to share physical acts is probably not possible.
- Sex is not something to be shared with just anyone. Yes, kissing is sex.
- When they do have a physical relationship, they should be aware that their physical needs should be met just like their emotional needs should be.
- With a sexual relationship, their health always comes first.
- I explained what STDs are.

- STDs are common among teenagers.
- Before they ever become physical with another person at any time during their lives, both they and their partner should both get full STD testing.
- Condoms do not fully protect us from transmission of STDs as so many people believe.
- Many people infected with STDs do not have symptoms and do not know they are infected, but they are still extremely contagious with no physical signs of disease.
- STDs are transmitted during oral sex, although many teenagers believe this is not possible.

Your children have more relationships than you can imagine, especially in this electronically connected world: friends, boyfriends, girlfriends, bosses, teachers.

You cannot micromanage any of it. Don't try. But you can instill in them the self-awareness that their needs must be considered in all relationships they have, especially romantic ones.

Teach them that if their needs are not met, don't fight it, and don't try to change the other person. Walk away.

CHILDREN AND TECHNOLOGY

Your Child's Cell Phone

Your children have a cell phone for your convenience.

A cell phone is not for your children's benefit.

It is a tool for you to communicate with them, keep track of them, and maintain schedules within your household. For your parenting purposes, your child's phone only needs to make phone calls and send text messages.

Many fathers don't know that to make phone calls and receive text messages, a cell phone does NOT need a data plan. The data plan is what gives a smartphone Internet access, and this is usually a very expensive monthly charge.

Our children have cell phones so we can call and text them. As parents, we don't derive many benefits from our children having a data plan on their cell phone.

Up until a child learns to drive, there is no need for him to have Internet access on his phone. When he begins driving, having Internet access can turn his smartphone into a navigation system, which I always wanted my children to have access to. However, the potential harm of a teenage child carrying Internet access in his pocket is huge. Please consider removing data plans from your children's phones until they are old enough to drive. Also, consider instituting some of the security measures detailed in this chapter.

Again, your child's phone does not need Internet access (a data plan) for you to call or text them.

A Lack of Knowledge

Part of the problem we have when trying to control our children's access to technology is a lack of knowledge.

There are so many components to technology today, it seems impossible to understand it all or to know where to start.

This lack of knowledge is one of the main problems parents need to overcome. Take a look at this next sentence:

**A Lack of Knowledge
leads to
A Lack of Confidence
leads to
Frustration, Fear, and Inaction.**

This can apply to so many areas of our lives, especially technology.

Technology is one of the few areas of our lives where our children's knowledge can exceed our own.

Most parents don't fully understand today's technology. If we did, then we would have much more confidence and actual know-how to control it.

Most cellular carriers offer the ability to restrict what appears on our phones. For example, you can restrict web browsers, iTunes, installation of new applications, and use of the phone's camera.

Verizon Wireless offers parental controls that are very easy to set for each of the phones on your plan. Most parents don't know about this. It is not perfect, but it can really restrict the information your children can see on their phones.

There are also other products you can buy that allow content filtering to protect your child from accidentally viewing something inappropriate.

As an added bonus, parents can now set restrictions that limit the ratings of movies, music, and podcasts children can access. Your cellular carrier's customer service department can walk you through this process.

I urge you to contact your cellular carrier and simply ask them what they offer for free to increase your family's cellular security.

Social Networking
Most of us use social networking programs.

Some may seem like innocent games, but many of them expose us to strangers, without restrictions.

If you give your children open access to the Internet, they will be able to see everything on the Internet—potentially harmful things like pornography, violent images, profanity, and music videos full of adult language and graphic sexual images. Adult strangers may be able to view pictures and steal your child's personal details. These adult strangers can sometimes easily contact your child.

I am often asked at what age a child should be allowed to have open and unsupervised access to the Internet. My answer? NEVER before fourteen, and then it depends on the child.

Technologically speaking, kids can run circles around their parents when it comes to using computers, but they don't know what to do when they get bullied or harassed or swindled. Often they can't even see it happening to them. This kind of thing can scar a person for life.

"Digital adulthood" is a result of unsupervised browsing and social networking that has the potential of surfacing "content and conversations that exceed the maturity of the user." I recommend that parents start talking to their kids and educating them about online dangers such as cyberbullying and sexual predators. Doing so will better prepare their kids to handle the real dangers of the digital world.

I also recommend parents consider installing Internet monitoring software.

To restate, the Internet is full of ADULT images and content. At what age should your child have access to adult images and content? Only you can decide, but I hope these words have made you more aware and more thoughtful about what is age-appropriate.

Video Gaming Consoles

An important warning here: many gaming consoles are now Internet connected and offer the same functionality to access the Internet as computers do.

I bring this up because it is an often overlooked device in the home. Most of us don't think a "video game" has anything to do with the Internet.

Usernames and Passwords

Your children have login information for all websites they use. I suggest keeping a master list of their usernames and passwords.

If your children refuse to share them, I would cut off access. Make no exceptions. I also suggest that all new "friends" be approved by you.

Let me tell you a Facebook story.

A friend of mine instituted these rules and tested her son's usernames and passwords by logging in to various websites every few days. One day she discovered that her son had changed his Facebook password. When he came home from school, he discovered an empty space where his computer used to be. He approached my friend, and before he said a word, it dawned on him what had happened. He did not get the computer back for thirty days, and during that time, he did his computer-related homework on the computer in his parents' room with their direct supervision.

Profile Information

Social networking sites have user profiles. Some of the most sensitive personal data are requested: phone numbers, birthdays, addresses, email contacts, etc. Take the time to go over these requested items with your children, and ask them to restrict how much personal information they share. Explain to them that there are predators in the world who can use this personal information to harm them.

Social Networking Privacy Warning

Maintaining privacy settings on social networking sites should be a top priority. What are privacy settings exactly?

Privacy settings allow a user to decide how much or how little information about them is available on a social networking site.

I urge you to become an expert on the privacy setting for all of the online networking/gaming sites your children access. Many of these sites will have a default setting of completely open information! What does this mean? This means that pictures your children post and messages they send may be accessible by total strangers on the Internet.

This is a very large problem, and parents have no idea how vulnerable and exposed their children are.

Many pictures today have exact GPS information embedded in them. This means that a picture posted online by your child will provide her exact location at the time the picture was taken. It is very easy for predators to create a detailed map of your child's whereabouts just using her pictures.

It is imperative that you gain control, which starts with gaining knowledge about your children's technological world.

Social Networking, Text Chatting, and Video Chatting
Most social networking sites have messaging and video chatting built in.

Without the proper safeguards, strangers can easily send messages or even engage in video chats with your children. Many smartphones have the ability to host video chat sessions as well. I cannot stress enough that we need to have the proper electronic restrictions in place to protect our children.

Home Network Security
What is really happening when we browse the web? Some of us do not know exactly what is going on. Understanding this is vitally important in our quest to manage teenagers and technology.

For most of us, the Internet comes into our homes from the same company with which we have cable TV service. So, we have a cable coming into our homes, and with that, an electronic link to the Internet is provided to us.

Usually, in our homes and at work, the Internet travels through a modem or a router first. This router/modem then will manage sharing that Internet signal with users in the home.

This simply means that for us to share that signal coming into our homes, we need a device to help us do that. Some computers and phones can connect wirelessly to your router, and some computers may be hard-wired.

Most people think that an Internet screen is like a TV picture, but it is slightly different.

A very important concept I want you to remember is that all the Internet data that you see on your computer or cell phone screens has to be downloaded onto that device before you see it.

Every letter and every picture is temporarily downloaded onto your computer or phone.

So, what can we do right away to make our home networks more secure? We can go into our router or modem settings and make some changes and increase our level of security.

1.   Content Filtering

There are many ways to control what data can flow to a cell phone or a computer. This is something most parents are not aware of. We can block certain websites or words if we want to. Let's say we want to block Facebook.com or CNN.com or certain words like "terrorism." We can do that within our modem/router settings.

This is called "content filtering."

When this is done correctly, instead of the desired website appearing on our child's screen, a warning message will appear instead stating that the website has been blocked.

That means that YOU get to choose what type of information will flow through your home network.

Now, there are ways around this, but we have to try to stay one step ahead of that if we can.

Remember, if your child has a web-enabled phone (data plan), he does not need to use your home router, and blocking sites in your router could be useless.

Many ISPs (Internet Service Providers) have great parental controls that you can use as well. You can block certain contents or sites at the source. Call your ISP to learn about these.

2.   We can actually assign times when the Internet is available in our home.

Wouldn't that be useful? So, it's 10 p.m., and you can be sure that no one can access the Internet until tomorrow.

3.   Password Security

Many home routers are NOT secure. What does this mean?

This means that anyone close enough to that router can gain access to your home network wirelessly. This is something you need to avoid. Identity thieves are out there, and they drive up and down streets looking for OPEN home networks to attack.

So, I urge you to learn how to password protect your home routers so only you and your family can access it.

It's ten p.m.; do you know who your children are talking/texting/sexting/video chatting with?

BUILDING FUNCTIONAL ADULTS FROM THE GROUND UP

Building functional adults who can be successful is the Foxhole Father's long-term goal.

I want my children to be able to cope with life's downturns and be functional in all areas of life:

- Academics
- Romance
- Athletics
- The Arts
- Spirituality
- Employment
- Parenthood
- Emotional Health

I want my children to quietly work hard and find success everywhere. I want my children to know and demand their value when accepting jobs. I want my children to be good neighbors and good citizens. I want them to be unimposing and unentitled. They were taught to respect the space of others, physically and emotionally.

I want their self-esteem and life satisfaction to come from their hard work and personal achievements only, ignoring all external criticisms and praise.

This includes ignoring my criticisms and praise.

It is important to differentiate between learning from mentors and others' experiences, and reacting to criticisms and praise.

In this context, criticisms and praise are usually the judgments of other people about things we have done. I find there is no value in either of these things. Learning from mentors is a completely different experience. We all have experiences on both sides of this. A good mentor will lovingly teach and be motivated by our best interests and achievements, just like a good parent will. I tried to teach my children how to tell the difference.

I have consistently tried to show them when they may be encroaching on someone else's space. This lesson has translated into them wanting their own space respected, which was my intention in the first place.

Remember, the behaviors and environments you reinforce will be viewed as normal and healthy to your children. When they are presented with the opposite, they will quickly recognize it and avoid it. This is the outcome you are working toward for them.

This conversation is expanded to include teaching them to not take advantage of others who are in a weakened position. They may come across psychologically weak individuals who have things to offer. If it can be shown that these things are being offered from a position of weakness and inequality in a relationship, then the children need to reject the offer.

The Foxhole Father teaches that in order to achieve their long-term goals, children will have do things they do not like or want to do. They will take classes they hate but still need to get the A. There will be functions at jobs they do not enjoy. They will have bosses and co-workers who are intolerable.

Impart to your children that successful people learn to do these unfulfilling things with the same vigor and emotional investment they have for things they love. Teach them to view the broader and future impact of their actions and realize how it can benefit them for years to come by acquiring this personality trait.

Teach them the benefits of delaying gratification now for long-term benefits in the future.

A good example of this is a high school freshman who hates Advanced Placement English. She knows that the basic-level English class would be a breeze. But she also knows that in three years, she will be applying to colleges. Taking that AP class now in freshman year might be the additional achievement she needs to be accepted into her college of choice a few years from now. So, although there is an easier option presented, she realizes that doing the harder and less comfortable work now can bring exponential benefits later.

A functional adult will have self-control and work harder and longer than others, knowing that in the long run, this can bring great rewards and job stability.

Your children can become fully functional adults in all areas.

It all starts with you, their Foxhole Father.

Their life's foundations are built with stones you provide.

What foundation are you giving your children?

QUESTION YOUR BELIEFS CONSTANTLY

The Foxhole Father questions the basis of his belief systems constantly. Some of our deepest convictions were simply placed within us by our parents or caregivers.

Your initial parenting instincts, based on these deepest of convictions, could lead to poor fathering.

Your fathering instincts may be based on dysfunctions that you learned at the hands of others. I am constantly searching for the genesis of the fathering I am about to share with my children.

- Why am I making a rule?
- Why am I making a suggestion?
- Why do I feel so strongly that what my child is doing or saying is wrong for them? Or right for them?
- Do these rules truly make sense in the context of my family unit and for this specific child's development?
- Am I sharing something that was ingrained in me as a youth?
- Am I breaking the main Foxhole Fathering rule and filtering my fathering through what is best for ME?
- Am I filtering my fathering through what will make ME comfortable?
- Am I attempting to quickly dispel MY fears?
- Do my gut reactions keep my children on the path to becoming strong, functional, and happy adults? You are flawed. We all are. This should be discussed openly with your children. Humanize yourself in their eyes. This does wonders for bringing your children close to you. Share the ideas in this chapter with them.

The Foxhole Father never acts omnipotent and all-knowing. Why?

This can make a child incapable of making his or her own decisions. Also, that type of parenting can create an emotional distance.

Along with questioning your belief systems, you should train yourself to include calmness, reflection, and pausing when parenting.

Prepare yourself by visualizing intense situations that may arise with your children in the future.

For example:

Let's say your child is struggling with a certain class. This has caused stress between the two of you. You are very angry at your child. You feel disrespected and hurt. This Friday, the weekly progress report will be brought home after school.

Your core beliefs tell you:

- Punishment must be enforced when there are bad grades.
- Bad grades equal disobedience and disrespect to you.
- Teachers have no fault if grades are bad.
- Your child should get good grades because you demand it.

These engrained beliefs can do damage.

In prior weeks, this waiting for the progress report has been excruciating for you, and it built up to an eruption on Friday afternoons. Every day, when your child comes home, she is stricken with fear and pressure and performance anxiety.

Your child sees your constant anger, judgment, and disappointment, even if you think you are concealing it. This pressure and anxiety will further hurt her grades.

For weeks now you have been saying judgmental things like:

- "What is wrong with you?"
- "How can you be so stupid?"
- "You are an embarrassment!"
- "Your brother got an A in that class!"
- "Don't bring home a bad progress report on Friday!"

These types of phrases and attitudes should never be part of your fathering, ever. Your beliefs have led you to attack your child, and your beliefs need to change immediately.

You can completely change your actions and reactions this week. You can make the Friday afternoon academic performance review only about your daughter and stop allowing your beliefs to guide your parenting.

Your new Foxhole Father beliefs can replace your existing ones.

Even beliefs we think are a permanent part of us can be peeled away and replaced with beliefs that are better for our children.

You can visualize what kind of father you want your child to have on Friday afternoon regardless of what the progress report says. You can choose to stop being an adversary to your child.

You are now filtering the situation in a new way, erasing your old beliefs.

You have eliminated judgments from your fathering.

You begin to think completely new ideas about the situation and realize the following ways you may have failed your child.

Have you:

- considered the idea that the teacher may be inadequate?
- met with the teacher to strongly reinforce his or her responsibility in supporting your child?
- requested a detailed analysis from that teacher on what your child's impediments might be in his or her class?
- reviewed your child's homework and study routine to see if you can suggest changes to increase his performance and understanding?
- made sure your child knows she has your full support and love?

Your original beliefs had you verbally attacking your child, and you became her adversary. She was living in fear of you and her grades.

Long ago, I personally chose to replace my core beliefs and stop judging my children. Instead, I began using the following supportive phrases:

- "I am here to help you with this 100%."
- "I know this is so difficult for you and that you are very frustrated, but we will figure this out together."

- "I know you are trying your best, so instead of working harder, let's work smarter."
- "Is there anything the teacher can be doing differently that would help you?"
- "Are you not able to follow the teacher's lessons? Do other classmates have the same issue?"
- "Maybe a tutor will help?"
- "I know you truly hate this class, but if you excel at this, you will be doing yourself a favor three years from now when you are applying to colleges."
- "Learning to take on challenges, like this class you hate, and doing them with the same passion for things you love, is one of the most important life lessons I can teach you."
- "I know you have a scheduled game this Saturday, but it is more important that I help you improve your grade in this class. So let's spend the weekend studying together."
- "This class and this grade do not define you as a person."

Objectively questioning your belief systems can lead to much better parenting.

YOUR DREAMS AND GOALS: WHAT IS THEIR EMOTIONAL BASIS?

I teach my children to strive for excellence, growth, and success in all areas. Before we can achieve true personal success, we need to find out what our internal goals are. Many people achieve great things, but they are emotionally unfulfilled because their motivation comes from someone or something outside of themselves.

So many of us allow things outside of us to impact our emotional state and give us unhealthy motivations. I call these "external definers."

What is an external definer? It can be so many things. One I have been a victim of is considering the happiness of others above my own. Other external definers can come from your significant other, your friends, your children, your parents, your co-workers, your church, etc.

This can lead to living a life in which you are constantly modifying your behavior and goals to satisfy someone else's definition of what you should be—living a life of enslavement to others.

Good examples of this are becoming a doctor because of your parents' expectations or maintaining a six-pack of abs because your girlfriend likes it.

This leads to a lack of peace in our lives as we are constantly trying to please others and keep them happy. It is impossible to satisfy all external definers, so we are never truly at peace with ourselves.

Too often our motivations are founded in insecurity, low self-esteem, and other dysfunctional self-images. There are many ways this happens to us. I have personally battled these things within myself. You may not have any idea what your internal dreams and goals are. This is not your fault.

The Foxhole Father seeks and destroys his external definers and only uses his internal motivations to guide his life's journey.

So many people attempt to achieve a goal, but very few truly analyze what their motivations are. This chapter encourages you to consider what your motivations and intentions are.

In order for us to teach our children to properly think about their motivations, we have to learn to do this for ourselves. Self-observation can be extremely difficult. Many people, when they discover they have been behaving in an unhealthy way for a long time, can be consumed with regret and self-loathing. Please avoid this! When you are self-observing, always be your own best friend. Many fathers feel terrible when they realize they have been influencing their children in harmful ways.

Don't turn these moments into self-criticism. Be proud that you are trying to become the best father you can be. That is all your children can ask of you, and it is a great success.

The more you discover the source of your motivations, the better father you will be.

Let's try an exercise together.

I would like you to list one important goal in your life, one from each of these categories:

- Hobbies
- Work
- Physical
- Emotional
- Spiritual
- Social

All of us should be able to think of one important goal within each of these categories. For example, one of your hobbies may be bowling, and your goal within that might be to bowl a perfect game. You may have very specific work goals. These may relate to your title, compensation, or sales goals. The last category is also the trickiest, and this is where people have the hardest time analyzing themselves. What type of social goals could we have? What does that mean exactly?

Social goals usually revolve around how we want the outside world to see us personally. This can mean maintaining a certain physique, owning a certain type of vehicle, engaging in certain activities, or being seen as having a certain level of expertise among a peer group.

Now that you listed a goal within each of these categories, I want you to take a step back, self-observe, and determine your motivations for them.

- What are the emotional, physical, or other tangible benefits you gain by achieving these goals?
- Do these benefits come from inside or outside of you?
- What are your motivations for having these goals?

The next step in this exercise is to imagine you suddenly stopped all efforts at achieving those goals, including any outward expression of these goals toward people in your life.

- How would this make you feel?
- What would be the initial impact on your life?
- How could this impact you physically, financially, and intellectually in the long run?
- Do any negative feelings that surface stem from things outside of you?
- Would you feel a sense of relief?

If you take your time with this exercise, and if you are very honest with your answers, this may give you great insight into yourself that you have not had before.

This exercise is meant to try to teach you how to self-observe. By doing this every day, you will be able to teach your children how to do this from a young age.

So many people are existing today, going moment to moment, trying to blindly satisfy others' expectations. This ignores our internal desires and goals. Very few people are deliberate about how they live their lives.

The Foxhole Father is deliberate about his life and actions. This gives him more control and success every day. The more you objectively observe yourself and analyze your motivations for what you are doing, the happier and more conscious you will be.

So many people seem to be less than conscious as they are going through their lives. They seem to be on a sort of autopilot, with no deliberate thought underlying their actions.

Many people spend endless energy maintaining others' perceptions of them.

We want our boss to think this about us, our wife to think that, and our friends to think something completely different. That is no way for a man to live. Try to self-observe when interacting with people and look at the emotional reasons for what you are doing and saying. Are you being evasive? Are you not being your true self? Are you nervous that your true nature will be discovered?

Are you simply making sure the other person is seeing the version of you that they want to see or expect?

If you are feeling any of these things, you don't necessarily have a problem. It is quite possible that the people with whom you are surrounding yourself are not good for you.

Are the people in your closest circles loving, caring, and nonjudgmental? Your wife, friends, co-workers? When you start to self-observe, this automatically increases your observations of those around you and how they treat you and how they live their lives.

These self-observations will lead you to a greater understanding of the emotional basis for your dreams and goals.

Having the courage to be your true self, regardless of the consequences, is the way I want my children to live. If I was constantly trying to keep up with the Joneses, or showing a great concern for what people thought of me, then my children would take on those same traits.

Your children are experts on you. They process and internalize everything you do. No one knows you better and no one observes you more than they do. To them, your goals and dreams and motivations will be normal, and they will copy them.

The Foxhole Father courageously presents his raw self to the world with no care for social acceptance.

Teach this lesson to your children. If you do, no matter what they go through in life, they will look for their happiness from within and never allow anything outside of themselves to negatively impact their emotions.

Your sense of personal accomplishment and self-worth should only come from within yourself.

I will discuss how I go through my days emotionally.

- I wake up and say a quiet prayer for those I love.
- I remind myself that I am not perfect, and perfection should never be expected of me or anyone.
- I do my best all day to take care of my responsibilities, fathering my children selflessly and serving my clients.
- When friction arises, I try to objectively discuss it and get to a better place if possible.
- When I go to bed, regardless of what people in my life may think or feel, if I have done my very best to love those around me, then I consider the day a complete personal success.

Now, my children, family members, or clients could all have negative feelings about me. But I cannot allow this to upset me. It is so easy to want popularity. Of course I don't want my children or family upset. Could I change my behaviors just to keep them happy with me? Of course, but that is at the heart of what external definers are. I need to be true to my personal motivations and desires.

I will discuss things objectively and lovingly, especially with my children. This is the best way to strengthen relationships. I want to understand why they are upset, and hopefully through discussion we can learn how to love and support each other even more.

The feelings of others are out of my control, and I don't worry what others' reactions will be. Again, I am not modifying my behaviors to make sure other people have certain emotions. My natural and internal motivations make me express my love and appreciation from the inside out.

External definers have no place in my self-image or my gauge of personal success and happiness.

Once you realize how many external definers you may be allowing to run your emotional system and your behavior, you will quickly try to dismantle these terrible impediments to your happiness.

Your children will learn this from you.

I can't think of a better Foxhole Fathering impact than that.

SPECIAL NEEDS CHILDREN

How does the Foxhole Father philosophy apply to special needs children?

Masculine nonjudgmental parenting carries forward to the parenting of a special needs child as well. The philosophy and mindset do not change.

Special needs children can be more physically and emotionally demanding. Don't allow your child's disability or impairment to become a barrier for him. He should see it as just another part of himself. Regardless of his special need, he can and should lead a full life.

The Foxhole Father of a special needs child has a challenging mission, but there is no doubt he can be victorious.

I do not have a special needs child, so I can't speak to the specific experiences of a father of a special needs child. However, I can explain the Foxhole Father's basic philosophy as it relates to fathering a special needs child.

The Foxhole Father of a special needs child does not shelter him.

He gives him the tools to lead a full and independent life.

If you believe that with hard work, courage, and selflessness, your children can achieve great things, then they will. Even if you are afraid, teach your child to push his or her limits. All children need real achievements to grow into functioning adults.

Special needs are varied, and I realize your child may have severe emotional and physical limitations.

Some parents shelter their special needs children out of fear for their physical well-being. They may want to shield their child from the emotional pain of judgmental and mocking stares. But these actions of sheltering are mostly based on the parents' worries.

The Foxhole Father eliminates his feelings from the equation and evaluates all situations based on what is best for his child. And what is best for his child? To become the most functioning and independent adult he can be and to need as little assistance as possible from others or society to live his life.

Teach him to never care what those outside of him may feel or say about him. Within this book you will hear this almost as a mantra. Teach your children to ignore the crowd's thoughts and peer pressure and to do what is best for them, only looking inside themselves to gauge their self-worth and sense of accomplishment. I know it is very difficult to not care what others think, but making them aware of their natural desire to seek approval from others will at least make them more able to deliberately and consciously put it in its proper emotional place.

So some parents need to get out of the way. They may be extremely afraid and feel their special needs child is too fragile or incapable.

If you show your children that you believe these things about them, they too will internalize these feelings.

If you show fear, they will learn and live fear.

Let's put the child first. What do we want? For our children to be as fully functioning as they can be. If you teach your children that you believe this and that no barrier is too great, they will believe it, and most importantly, they will achieve or exceed it.

Here are stories of remarkable fathers of special needs children who have honored me by including their Foxhole Father stories in this book.

SARAH JANE'S STORY
By Patrick Donohue, father of Sarah Jane Donohue

Being the parent of a child with special needs is special! My nine-year-old daughter, Sarah Jane, was born perfectly healthy; however, when she was only five days old, her baby nurse violently shook her in the middle of the night, breaking four ribs and both collarbones, and causing a severe brain injury (she lost about 60% of the rear cortex of her brain). While she cannot walk on her own or speak words yet, one day she will. And it is my job to change the world for her. As the father of a special needs child, it is your job to change the world for your son or daughter, too. My goal is to give you some guidance on how to do this.

First of all, there are five key concepts:

1. Daily philosophy: Things work out best for those who make the best of the way things work out!
2. You are not alone.
3. Your child's special needs impact not just your child, but your entire family.
4. Be tone deaf to the word, "No."
5. Your child only has one daddy!

Things Work Out Best for Those Who Make the Best of the Way Things Work Out

By now you may have heard the beautiful story "Welcome to Holland," by Emily Perl Kingsley, about a woman who was planning the trip of her life to visit Italy. She had spent countless hours dreaming about the trip and making arrangements to experience all of the incredible sights, sounds, and tastes of Italy. However, when she got off the plane, she found herself in Holland instead of Italy, and she was stuck there for the rest of her life! As you can imagine, she was shocked, angry, and distressed with the unintended change in her plans. As she got settled into her circumstances, she found that Holland has many wonderful things to enjoy and appreciate. She explains she will always have disappointments about never visiting Italy, but she realized that if she spent all of her time being upset, she wouldn't enjoy her new experiences in Holland.

I recommend you read the entire story if you haven't already. This story highlights the most important philosophy I can share with you, "Things work out best for those who make the best of the way things work out!" Whenever I have moments of sadness, despair, regret, or hopelessness, I immediately return to this philosophy, and it snaps me back to happiness and hopefulness!

You Are Not Alone

Even with the rarest disorders for children, there are others who have the same or similar experiences as your child and your family. It is important you find a local, national, or international support group that deals with the same issues. There is no reason to reinvent the wheel. There is a wonderful expression, "Wise men learn from their mistakes, fools never do, and geniuses learn from the mistakes of others!" The key is to be as foolish as few times as possible, as wise as often as possible, and have as many moments of genius as you can. A simple way to do this is to find others who have already walked in your shoes. One of the key lessons you will learn from others who have had similar experiences is for you to not blame yourself. There are also other local sources of support you should seek out for help including religious and civic organizations. As I started a worldwide novena (a special Catholic prayer) to Mother Teresa to get Sarah Jane walking and talking, I explained that I was not relying upon science alone to change the world for her. Whatever faith or spiritual guidance you practice, I urge you to use it as a foundation for hope. I tell people all of the time to keep the prayers coming—they work!

Your Child's Special Needs Impact
Not Just Your Child, but Your Entire Family

During the acute phase of finding out about the challenges your child is facing, it is very easy to ignore the rest of your family. Unfortunately, the trauma also negatively impacts the marriage and siblings, and these concerns are usually not addressed. Do not make this mistake. You should immediately seek counseling for your marriage and your children. Hospitals have social workers who are specially trained to help the family. Take advantage of them as a resource. And once you leave the hospital, be sure to continue with marriage and family therapy. The future is going to be very difficult for you and your family; however, if you are not careful, these difficulties can lead to divorce and emotional challenges for your other children. You need to set the example as the man of the family and show that it is stronger to ask and seek help than "tough it out." Your wife and children will be very thankful you were proactive in this regard. If you are already divorced, you should still seek counseling for yourself and your other children to provide a safe place to talk about the many feelings you will experience.

You will also find that many family members and friends may have difficulty speaking with you or they may ignore you altogether. Do not chase after anyone who is not supportive. This is an opportunity for you to see who your real friends are and for you to find new friends who will be supportive and understanding. If someone offers you help—take it!

Be Tone Deaf to the Word "No"

The systems of care for many childhood illnesses are arbitrary from state to state, random from school district to school district, and illogical from one doctor's office to another. There is an ironic tendency for these systems that are supposed to help your child and family to actually create roadblocks—whether it is the Medicaid office creating piles of paperwork for you to fill out just to get services your child is entitled to receive, or the school district not spending the necessary time to understand the needs of your child and ensure there are adequate accommodations for your child to receive a Free and Appropriate Public Education (it's referred to as FAPE and is federally required).

There are professionals who work with families who have children with special needs; be sure to seek out their support. These systems can be overly complex and confusing, so it helps to talk with families in your support group to find those resources and utilize them. Do not be too "proud" to seek support from the systems that are designed to help you and your family. This is what your tax dollars are supposed to be spent on. There may be times you need to seek legal help. Do not be afraid to do so; just make sure you get help from professionals who are experts in their field. For example, in the field of brain injury, there are many personal injury attorneys who will take a case but do not know anything about brain injury. However, there are wonderful attorneys who specialize in Brain Injury Law and know more than many doctors. A great resource for legal advice is the National Disabilities Rights Network (www.NDRN.org). They have chapters in all fifty states, and this is the perfect place to start if you are having problems with the systems designed to help your child and your family. Another great resource that deals with the area of special education is Wrights Law Forum (www.WrightsLaw.com).

Besides the governmental systems, the medical systems are very difficult to navigate. Many childhood diseases deal with neurologic conditions (i.e., brain injury caused by trauma or non-trauma such as strokes, brain tumors, epilepsy, or other conditions like autism, ADHD, and rare genetic disorders). Since we only know about 5% of what we will eventually know about the brain (never mind the developing brain), stay away from doctors or others who tell you things "definitively." Think about how much we knew about heart disease in the 1850s; that's about as much as we know about the brain today. My daughter's first pediatric neurologist tried to define what she would or wouldn't be able to do for the rest of her life before she was even one month old! We fired him and found an incredible, caring doctor whose mantra was simply, "We will not create false expectations for Sarah Jane, but we will never give up hope!" In all the years and with the many doctors, therapists, and teachers I have come to know, I can assure you the overwhelming majority of them have the same hopeful attitude. These are walking angels on the planet; surround your child and your family with these amazing people. Remember, it is our responsibility to advocate for our children. These angels wake up every day and choose to help our kids and our families—be sure to thank them every chance you get!

Your Child Only Has One Daddy

Remember, at the end of the day, there is only one man on the planet who cares about your child more than himself—that is his or her daddy! If you do not advocate as hard as possible for your child and your family, you cannot expect anyone else to do so. If you set the example, people will notice and the systems will respond better to you. Try not to reinvent the wheel; instead, learn from others' experiences. However, if you find out the wheel for your child hasn't been invented yet or needs to be improved—do it! They say the wheel started off as a square stone, and as the cavemen pushed it, the edges continued to shave off until it was round. Don't stop pushing the stone for your child—it is your job!

I have yet to find one special needs condition where the systems run perfectly and all of the answers have already been figured out. Some are better than others, but you need to fight very hard for your child. As the only daddy your child will ever have, it is your responsibility to be the voice for your child. As you read through this book, you will see a common theme—taking responsibility for the nurture and development of your child. I will not sugarcoat it and say it is easier to do this for a child with special needs. But I will tell you the trip to Holland is filled with wonderful, beautiful moments of laughter and tears, but mostly HOPE! Remember: Things work out best for those who make the best of the way things work out!

JAKE'S STORY
By Fred Chalmers, father of Jake Chalmers

Before I begin the story of Jake, I want to briefly set the stage. Our family gene pool is outstanding. Our family history is one of athletic skill and health. I was raised to work hard, take risks, and make no excuses.

The date was September 6, 1990. I had twins, a boy and a girl who were six-years-old and already showing signs that the athletic genes are very inherent. They were bright and beautiful.

Jake was born, and all was wonderful with the feeling of excitement and joy of another perfect child joining our perfect family.

While my wife was recovering, a doctor tapped me on the shoulder and asked me to step out of the room. "What's going on, Doc?" I asked.

"Well, your son Jake has Down Syndrome. We will have someone from our staff explain this to help you better understand the situation."

Much of this moment in time is still a blur (I was dazed and confused), but I will try to explain my feelings about that day as honestly as I can.

The hospital was obviously bright and well lit, but what I remember is slumping down in a hallway of the hospital, which to my recollection was empty and dark. I was holding my hands over my face, crying and totally numb. Thousands of thoughts were running through my mind: "This can't be true!" "What am I going to do?" "Can I handle this?

Questions that kept running through my head were:

- Will other kids mock and make fun of him?
- Will other kids mock and make fun of the twins?
- How will the twins handle this, and will they be embarrassed or

afraid of Jake?

- Will my adult friends be uncomfortable around Jake and/or treat him differently?
- How do I tell my friends and colleagues? What will their reaction be, pity?
- How will I keep it together if I witness someone being cruel to Jake? (I truly feel I would and could hurt someone very badly if this occurred.)
- How could this happen to me and my wife?

Over the next few days and weeks I heard the word "special" until I wanted to scream. I felt it was a term someone came up with to make a bad situation sound better.

Then my dad said to me, "Everything will work out fine; you just need to set different goals and objectives."

Fast forward twenty-three years.

Every night when I lie in bed, the same questions and fears run through my mind ... every night! But before I fall asleep, I remind myself that it was yet another outstanding day filled with joy, love, and accomplishments. Yes, twenty-three years ago, 8,395 days of joy, love, and accomplishments. Jake is the most amazing kid you could ever meet and makes everyone around him a better person.

The word "special" is not a word created to make something sound better, but the perfect word to describe Jake. Every day he brings a smile to everyone he comes in contact with. I truly believe Jake thinks he is the most important person in the world and that everyone and everything revolves around him.

So how did we get to this point?

First off, Jake has gone and goes everywhere with us. He is exposed to everything our family is exposed to. He experiences everything the traditional family experiences. No boundaries.

We set goals for Jake that are challenging but achievable.

School work and grades are addressed and discussed. Homework was done by 8:00 p.m. each night or else!!

Chores need to be completed each and every day. Yes, he has chores. Outside of cutting the grass (safety concerns), there is nothing around the house that Jake can't do or hasn't done. He loves to be challenged and takes pride in all his accomplishments. He thrives on making us proud of him.

Jake has been a member of the Challengers Youth Association for over fifteen years. The CYA is a sports league for children with disabilities. We motivate Jake to practice and improve his skills. We let him know when we feel there was a lack of effort. We push him to be the best he can be.

The CYA has been a godsend to Jake and all the other kids who participate. I have always been an advocate of sports, knowing there is no better venue to teach kids life skills and life lessons. Jake's self-esteem and confidence have been impacted dramatically because of this experience.

Our family rule is we make no excuses for Jake and hold him accountable for his actions. His brother and sister have no problem getting on his case when he steps out of line. We do not shelter or enable Jake and don't allow any outside forces to do so, either.

Jake has experienced and been right in the middle (on many occasion) of his brother and sister's sports celebrations and championships. He's been a member of a wedding party, marched with his graduating Middletown South High School senior group, sits on the bench as a member of a high school basketball coaching staff, thrown out the first pitch at a professional baseball game, participates every year in the Special Olympics, and teaches us something new on the computer every day. Jake works a full-time job four days a week now, and you cannot talk him into missing a day, no way and for no reason.

Jake's life is full and rich. All his brother's and sister's friends from high school through college are Jake's friends. His phone book is bigger than the yellow pages. All of our friends are Jake's friends. There is very little Jake has not experienced as he continues to touch so many lives. We have allowed Jake the space and latitude to live his life to the fullest. We have allowed him the freedom to make mistakes.

Jake is very self-sufficient and terribly independent (almost to a fault). Yes, we do have a special eye out for him, but we also know there are another couple hundred other people out there with a special eye out as well. We cannot imagine a world without Jake in it. Jake has been called the "Mayor of Middletown" by so many as he moves effortlessly through the town.

How foolish and embarrassed I feel for what I was thinking on September 6, 1990.

I will conclude with a quick story that happened very recently and captures who Jake is today.

It was the day before Mother's Day, and Jake and I were having lunch with my parents. At the table, my dad gave Jake ten dollars and told him to remind me before we came back tomorrow to celebrate Mother's Day to pick up three bags of ice. As is customary, Jake excused himself and went upstairs to play on the computer (con-artist), or so we thought.

Unbeknownst to us, Jake had quietly left the house (shrewd) and was headed to the local Quick Check, approximately 300 yards away (independent). Not more than twenty minutes later, he walked into the kitchen, sweating terribly and carrying three bags of ice (amazing). Yes, he walked into Quick Check, retrieved the ice, and went to the counter and paid for it. He wanted to do something nice. He wanted to show he could handle it. He wanted us to be proud of him. Mission accomplished.

If you are wondering if I was upset he left the house without telling us and traveled quite a distance by himself, the answer is yes, very much so, and I let him know it. But at the same time, I was bursting with pride.

I have applied the masculine nonjudgmental advice you will find outlined in this book. If you have a special needs child, I urge you to do the same.

WHEN YOUR CHILD IS BEING BULLIED

Conflict vs. Bullying: Bullying is not a phase young people must endure or outgrow. Bullying is not a conflict between students or among groups of students. Conflict is a mutually competitive or opposing action or engagement, including a disagreement, an argument, or a fight, which is a normal part of human development. Bullying is one-sided, where one or more students are victims of one or more person's aggression, which is intended to physically or emotionally hurt the victim(s).

From the moment you hear about a bullying incident from your child, you need to be his or her advocate. It is in these moments that your Foxhole Fathering will help build strength within your children, teach them vital life skills, and build an even stronger bond between the two of you.

1. In many states, bullying is a criminal act.
2. You should never directly confront the person whom your child has accused of bullying him or her.
3. Your first step here is to lovingly assure your child that you are going to do everything you can to protect him and to make the bullying stop. It is critical that you approach this situation calmly. Your child may already be traumatized, and if your reactions are emotionally charged, even if you have good intentions, this may make the situation worse for your child. Let him talk openly and describe exactly what is happening without interruption. Let him know you completely understand what is happening and that there is no weakness in what he is going through. Try to speak in pacifying tones. In these situations, it is very common for a parent to get very scared for his child. This is completely natural, but you need to avoid expressing your personal feelings at this

moment. What is important here is fathering your child through this situation. As I discuss often in this book, your feelings and personal reactions usually serve no positive purpose and should not be expressed at these moments.

4. Calmly write down notes from your child as to exactly what has happened, how long it has been happening, and how it makes your child feel. Gather all the evidence you can: witness lists, emails, texts, or chat logs. This is very good to have in case you need to file a police report. Your child may be much more open with you than with school personnel or the police, so take your time building an evidence file before bringing in other parties. Make sure to find out if your child has expressed these problems to any school employee. If so, find out who and when, and request copies of any paperwork completed and the details of any conversations that person has had with your child. The more you learn, the better equipped you will be to direct the best outcome for your child.

5. Many school districts have implemented formal anti-bullying protocols in which the process is handled in a mediative way. I believe these protocols have their benefits, but there may be instances where the police should be involved and criminal charges brought against the bully. You may need a formal restraining order against the bully so he or she is forced to avoid your child. You need to direct this entire process on your child's behalf. When bullying occurs in a school environment, you may find that the school administrators do not want to get the local police involved. You may need to ignore that. Bullying is a form of assault, and it should be viewed that way. When the bullying involves physical contact of any kind, I recommend that parents file a police report first. School administrators may want to handle things privately and avoid any outside scrutiny. Remember, YOU are the main educator of your child, not a principal, teacher, guidance counselor, or police officer. You know what is best for your child. Don't ever let anyone tell you they know the best course of action for your child, especially in a bullying situation.

6. There are many forms of bullying, some more blatant than others.

Bullying can be physical, verbal, social and emotional, or cyber. There are so many possible ways for our children to be bullied today. If you are the masculine nonjudgmental place for them, there is a better chance your children will to come you when they have a problem.

7. Many children suffer from bullying in silence and for much longer than is necessary. Look for even slight behavior changes in your children. Each child who is bullied can show it in different ways. If your instincts tell you something is wrong with your child, keep communicating with him or her until you get to the bottom of it. This may take time and patience, but don't give up.

When many of us were in middle school and high school, today's Internet and social media connectivity did not exist. Bullying back then was much more exposed, and the types of bullying were much fewer. Please be mindful of this fact and learn about today's electronic social environments. Today's bullies have many more options and more chance to remain anonymous.

One way to minimize bullies' access to your children is by not giving your teen a web-enabled smartphone. That is discussed in the section, "Children and Technology," page 135.

It might be beneficial to get your bullied child in therapy, depending on the severity of what he has been through. Many children will tell you everything is OK, when in actuality there is still tremendous turmoil and emotional upset just under the surface.

What if your child is the bully? That also is a good time to consider therapy for your child and objectively analyze your parenting methods. Bullies and predators are molded over time in dysfunctional home environments.

Regardless of the situation, the Foxhole Father completely controls the process and structures the best outcomes for his child.

DO NOT BE IMPAIRED OR TAKE DRUGS
IN FRONT OF YOUR CHILDREN

The Foxhole Father is never impaired in front of his children.

I want you to imagine you are eight years old. You are four feet tall and weigh fifty-five pounds. Your arm is bleeding heavily, and you run in the house from the backyard. You look down, and your shirt and pants are soaked with blood. You are crying, hyperventilating, and screaming for your father.

Suddenly in front of you is a 250-pound, six-foot five-inch tall man. He is trying to say your name, "Timmy," but it is coming out like "Sssttsssiiimmmeee." He is wobbling from side to side and sometimes leaning up against the wall. His eyes are not fully open, and they are beet red. He is holding a brown bottle in his hand, and his shaky other hand is trying to grab you.

This monster looks like your father, but what stands before you is not him.

Your eight-year-old mind tries to process the many terrors you are feeling.

- What happened to my dad?
- Who did this to him?
- How much blood do I have left in my body?
- Why can't he say my name?
- Will he always be this way?
- What if he falls and gets hurt?
- What if he falls on me?
- I need help right now; who will protect me?
- Am I going to die?

When you are impaired in front of your children, and they have a serious need, know that these terrors are running through their minds. Imagine their terror when they need you and the father they know is gone.

The last terror in that list would read, "When will he be this way again?" The anticipatory anxiety a child can feel waiting for the next time their father will be impaired is excruciating. Don't put your children through this. It is one childhood terror you can completely shield them from.

Have you ever been impaired by drugs or alcohol around your small or teenaged children? I want you to reread the scenario above, and I want you to really self-observe. I want you to make a commitment to your children that you will never let that happen again.

Your children could have smaller non-life-threatening "emergencies," and if you are impaired, their terrors could still be the same as those listed above.

You have children; your life is not your own. You have to be the man they need in every situation. That man does not wobble and slur his words. That man is ready to safely drive them to the emergency room at all times.

I am not advocating removing alcohol from your life. I am saying that drinking to the point where you are physically and verbally altered in front of your children is a mistake, and it can hurt them.

The emotional and psychological damage can be life altering. To me, alcohol is a drug. Think of the life lesson you teach when you are impaired by drugs or alcohol. You are showing your children that you are not comfortable with your natural state and that you need a drug to change it. I never wanted my children to see that as a normal behavior, so I have never been impaired around them. Show them you don't need drugs or alcohol to be part of your leisure time.

The Foxhole Father is consistent. You are their benchmark. What you show them will become their definition of a man for the rest of their lives.

If you need to "relax," then just do it when your children are long asleep. In the morning, when they come and wake you up to start their day, you will be the same father who tucked them in the night before.

They deserve a stable and consistent father every minute of every day. Give that to them from this moment on.

ROMANTIC PARTNERS ARE OPTIONAL; CHILDREN ARE YOUR LIFE'S WORK

Your romantic partner may be your perfect life partner, but she may be an incompatible co-parent. I believe this happens more often than people think or care to admit.

Your children need to get your fathering unfiltered. This means that there is a clear communication channel between you and them at all times, and there is always one clear parenting message.

What if your partner does not share your parenting vision on significant issues?

What if your partner adopts lifestyles that contradict yours?

I call these co-parenting static.

Some men may be silent, even though they disagree with what is happening in their homes. Some men may believe that a mother knows best. This lack of confidence can hurt your children.

Your silence and inaction are fathering mistakes. Don't make them.

The Foxhole Father is a hands-on father.

Children need their father's parenting guidance every day—his masculine nonjudgmental guidance.

You cannot ignore significant parenting and lifestyle differences, as your children's healthy development is at stake.

Do all you can to come to agreements on parenting with your children's mother. If you don't, the children will receive mixed messages in their home, and that can lead to disaster.

The first step is to have private discussions with their mother on the parenting or lifestyle issue at hand. Both of you need to calmly explain your view and why it is best for the children in the long run. Truly listen to each other objectively. Be prepared to learn things from each other. You have different experiences and parenting skills; use these to your children's advantage. The best parenting is collaborative in nature, and your parenting should blend into one transparent message. That is the dream situation.

Sometimes you will find that only one of you has deeply analyzed your parenting direction. In those cases, that parent's direction might be the best to take, as he or she has given the situation the most thought and is emotionally invested. The other parent may simply be having a surface knee-jerk reaction to a situation.

Both of your parenting options should be evaluated based on the short- and long-term impacts they may have on your child. If you both respect each other and put your children's development first, then most times you will come to a strong joint decision and then present that to your children.

But what if your parenting on many significant issues is completely different? What if your partner is making lifestyle choices that contradict your own? This can be so confusing for children.

Imagine that at work you had two bosses with the exact same authority over you.

Boss 1 comes out of her office and gives you the office rules and dress code. Five minutes later, Boss 2 comes out and gives a completely different set of rules and dress code. You have to obey their rules equally, although that is impossible.

Now, what if that happened all day, every day? Confusion, chaos, and anxiety, right?

Now, imagine what a five-year-old feels living in a household with two equal parents giving her different parenting direction every day.

Do not let this happen.

All too often, fathers feel helpless when the mother makes a significant parenting decision they disagree with. If you are in this position, you need to wake up. Your children's futures are at stake, and they need their father's presence more than ever.

If you cannot come to agreement on significant parenting issues, then please seek out marriage counseling to try to get on the same page.

If counseling doesn't bring you both to a unified parenting message, then you may need to consider separating from your children's mother and creating your own home. It is impossible to be an effective father in a home with a partner whose parenting philosophies or personal lifestyle are extremely different from your own.

Remember, your romantic partner may be your perfect life partner, but she may be an incompatible co-parent.

Romantic partners are optional; children are your life's work.

If you do separate, I urge all fathers to demand equal parenting time (overnights) in any child-sharing arrangement. Don't let anyone or anything persuade you against this. Always get the sharing arrangement in writing. The children should have the benefit and influence of both parents equally.

If you remain together, your children will believe that you agree with their mother's views and lifestyle choices, no matter what you do or say. If your differences are severe, do not fool yourself into believing that you can stay and still be an effective father. You do not want to have parenting battles in front of your children on a regular basis. Remember Bosses 1 and 2 above?

Don't make the mistake of believing that you can change your partner's views to yours. That is mostly impossible. She needs to be respected for her parenting and lifestyle choices, just as you want to be.

Establishing your own homes may be the only way for both of you to parent your children effectively. That is what you want to achieve at all times. If you can have that while living with their mother, that is ideal, but it is not always possible.

When you are living alone with your children, they will no longer see you as a parenting unit. You will no longer be seen as condoning decisions and lifestyles you disagree with. Your children will get your fathering unfiltered without co-parenting static. That is best for them, always. Their mother can now do the same.

To continue our work analogy above, the employee now has two places of business, each with its own boss and rules, with no overlap.

Ah, that's much better.

And now, from a distance, you can help your children navigate what is happening in their mother's home.

Remember, regardless of your living arrangements, your children need your unfiltered fathering. Never compromise this. Ever.

Eliminate co-parenting static.

Romantic partners are optional; children are your life's work.

FOXHOLE STEPFATHER

I have never been a stepfather, so I cannot fully understand that experience.

I do know many stepfathers. Some seem to be of significant benefit to their stepchildren, but others are perceived as an intrusion and interloper.

Stepfathers are some of the most giving and selfless people I have ever met and often take stepchildren into their hearts in ways that rival a biological parent's love.

In some ways, a Foxhole Stepfather's responsibilities exceed those of a biological father. If the two main Foxhole Father philosophies are followed, stepfathers can be a great part of their stepchildren's lives. Those are:

- "What is best for my (step)child?" comes before the stepfather's needs.
- Be a masculine nonjudgmental sanctuary for your stepchild.

A stepfather, like a biological parent, must believe that his needs and feelings do not matter and never inject those into parenting situations.

Stepfathers can play a great role, but quite often that opportunity is missed due to a lack of understanding of how stepchildren perceive them.

Unfortunately, many adults make the decision to cohabitate before fully considering their children's needs. Some parents cohabitate even with open opposition from their children.

My first advice to stepfathers is to be ever conscious that they are a stranger living with someone else's children. The children have a biological parent who is in charge of the household. My second advice is to wait until a stepchild asks you for help and advice before you offer it. Always suggest that the biological parents should be the first place a child should seek direction on significant issues.

The Foxhole Stepfather:

- realizes his stepchildren decide his true position naturally, over time.
- must understand that true position so he does not encroach or overstep at any time into his stepchild's space.
- does not attempt to enforce what he believes his position should be.
- realizes that his presence is unnecessary and possibly detrimental to his stepchildren's development.
- defers to the biological mother and father for all significant issues.

Healthy and effective parental authority cannot simply be "installed" in a home like a dishwasher.

Stepchildren's feelings about their stepfather can vary in the extreme. He can be seen as a roommate who sleeps with their mother and steals her attention, or a vital masculine role model that helps them become functioning adults.

The Foxhole Stepfather realizes the place he holds in his stepchildren's hearts evolves slowly.

Have you ever heard of an adult child in therapy at thirty years of age whose emotional issue is:

"My mother never got remarried! Why didn't she give me a stepfather and stepbrothers and stepsisters?"

Of course not. I don't believe it has ever happened.

I don't tell you these things to discourage you; quite the contrary. I am hoping to give you a perspective that can make your existing or soon-to-be stepfather role easier. I want to remove pressure you may feel to suddenly become a fully responsible additional parent for your partner's children. You don't have to. Stepfathers have great intentions and want to make a difference in their stepchildren's lives. But let your place in those children's lives grow slowly from an evolution, not a sudden revolution.

The Foxhole Stepfather treads lightly and silently, but is always ready to be of service when called upon.

Remember, your stepchildren have been forced to live with you. Try to imagine this from their perspective and how they may perceive you. If you never became their stepfather, there would no negative consequence to them. Conversely, the potential discomfort and long-term harm you can cause is exponential.

With no negative consequence to the children as a baseline, and using my philosophy of putting children first, the most conservative thing to do is to not force children to live with a stepfather.

So do your best to be a nonintrusive masculine nonjudgmental sanctuary at all times.

If a stepfather has been the only father a child has known since birth, then he may be perceived as the biological father would, heading the household along with the mother. That can be of great benefit for that child.

Even in that situation, if the biological father is active, the stepfather should take a secondary and supporting role and defer to the biological parents.

If a stepfather comes into a situation after the stepchildren have reached a certain age, I think it is very hard for him to attain the same position in the home's hierarchy that a biological parent can, and he should not try to.

This subordinate role can be very hard to accept for some men. But remember your personal feelings do not matter. Stepchildren should not have to accommodate a stepfather in any way. They have been forced to cohabitate with him based on their mother's needs.

Is your presence in their home causing problems? Please do all you can to minimize this immediately. Your stepchildren's needs come first, and they deserve a peaceful home. Regardless of the reason, if your presence is impacting their lives in a negative way, you may have to consider moving out to remove this detriment from their lives.

Their healthy development comes first, and a peaceful home life should be provided at all costs. Your romantic needs should never be considered ahead of your stepchildren's developmental needs.

Are you injecting your opinions into disagreements between your stepchildren and their mother? Are you sure that you have earned that level of trust and authority in their lives? If not, stepfathers should remove themselves from these situations. It is hard to accept, but most intense parenting situations are none of a stepfather's business, and he can do more harm than good.

The Foxhole Stepfather has been given a great gift and responsibility. If he approaches his stepfatherhood as a Foxhole Stepfather, he can become a cherished and respected mentor.

My mother married her husband Dominick when I was in my mid twenties. He is a significant part of my life and my children's lives. We are truly blessed to have him.

Dominick is my example of what a Foxhole Stepfather should be. The following description of him summarizes the best possibilities in this chapter.

Dominick is ever mindful to not encroach where he may not be welcomed, but he nurtures my family constantly. His selfless interactions and respect for our needs, over time, elevated him to a position of the greatest respect and love in our hearts.

Foxhole Stepfathers, following Dominick's example will serve your family well.

SECTION 3

FOXHOLE SINGLE FATHER

Although this section is called Foxhole Single Father, I urge all fathers to read it. There are important concepts included here from which coupled fathers can benefit.

Whether coupled or single, first read it for yourself, and then immediately share it with single fathers you know so they can join us in the Foxhole.

FOXHOLE SINGLE FATHER

TABLE OF CONTENTS

LETTER TO FOXHOLE SINGLE FATHERS

Dear Foxhole Single Father:

I have been a single father since 1997, so know I can relate to many things you are going through now and will experience for years to come.

When you became a Foxhole Single Father, you and your children started a completely new and unknown phase of your lives. Even if you are still living with their mother, she is now your ex, and she will forever occupy a different place in your life and your children's lives.

Every step you take from now on must be deliberate, focused, and come from a basis of strength, confidence, and conviction. If you show your children anything less than this, they could suffer in the long run. You will make mistakes. I made so many. Don't dwell on them; just learn from them, go forward, and do your very best.

Read these preliminary action items and then please read the full chapters in this Foxhole Single Father section.

You need to be proactive and physically present in all areas of your children's lives.

If you have not been present and a full participant in your children's lives, you should make a life change at this moment and establish a proper commitment and priority for the rearing and nurturing of your children. You may not know how to do this, and that is what this book is for. I will help you understand many issues you now face, and if you take my advice, your children will benefit from this for the rest of their lives.

What is best for your children must come first.

Child-sharing arrangements may not always work for your children.

A child's need to spend time with either parent is fluid and changing. What may work today may not work for your children a year from now. Please be aware of this and be open to temporary changes based on what your children need. Ask your ex to have the same flexibility. Your children should never feel that your sharing arrangement absolutely dictates when they can see either of you.

Personal feelings about your ex should not be considered when making fathering decisions. If she puts your children first and lives for them as you do, then be thankful and work to foster that every day. No matter what happened between you, you both had equal part in your failed relationship. No one is wrong; you are wrong for each other. Don't define yourself by what happened there. Forgive her and move on. Hopefully she will do the same.

Often I see people making parenting decisions based on spite and a desire to hurt their ex.

A good example: No matter how you have tried to structure sharing time, your children may want to be with their mother during "your" time. Those of you with animosity toward your children's mother may allow this to influence your decision, and you may automatically disallow it. This breaks the rule of filtering everything through the question, "What is best for my child?" If you take your personal feelings out of it and you find that your child will benefit from being with his or her mother during your time, then you should give permission happily.

Was I always able to do this? Of course not. My ex and my children witnessed my pettiness and selfishness at times. I am trying to help you learn from my mistakes.

Always be the first option to have your children.

What does this mean? If it is your children's mother's day to have them and she is unable to physically be with them, you need to be given the option above all others to watch the children for her. That means priority over her family, babysitters, or friends. Get this in writing. She deserves the same priority. Your children are always better off being with their parents whenever possible. Getting this in writing may help ensure this happens.

When you need help, ask someone!

There are many people in your life to whom you have been a good friend or brother. This is one time in your life when everyone around you needs to help you as much as possible. Being a single father can leave a man extremely insecure, and pride can get in the way of reaching out to others for help. There is NO embarrassment in seeking assistance and support during this time.

Creating a new home for your children by yourself may be one of the most stressful and frightening things you will ever do. It can quickly exhaust you, physically and emotionally.

You are not alone. Prove it to yourself by reaching out to those who love you when you need anything.

Communicate your contact information to people/institutions entrusted with your children.

There is a larger chapter dedicated to this topic in Section 2 of this book called "School/Activities – You are the Main Educator of Your Children," page 115. I suggest you read that as well.

You should prepare a complete list of all doctors, schools, and activity locations for your children and communicate your contact information to them. You should explain that there will be, or has been, a separation and that you expect the institution in question to communicate with you on all matters related to your children. This includes phone calls, emails, regular mailings, and text messaging. Make sure that you are listed as a co-main contact.

Many institutions deal with mothers almost exclusively, and so they assume that the mother is the main and only point of contact. You need to be patient and not adversarial. These attitudes are not personal, and you should never take them that way. When there is severe discord with your ex, it is very easy for you to maintain a high level of emotional stress that can easily come out at innocent people when discussing your children. It is imperative that you consciously self-observe and maintain control of yourself. Try to not allow any personal anguish and anger that you may feel come to the surface in any interactions that relate to your children. If your ex was at fault in the breakup, put it behind you. You are no longer together, so move forward and build the best co-parenting relationship with her that you can.

If you are in a bad mood, you may want to delay making certain phone calls or sending emails or text messages, especially to your ex.

Create a completely new fathering definition.

You CAN present the YOU to the world that you choose to. The rest of your life is a clean slate, and old patterns and dysfunctional relationships do not have to impact you any longer. You are now free to establish a home for your children based on your unique parenting vision. You are now free to become the father that your children truly need and who will be the best masculine and nonjudgmental person they will ever know. You do not have to answer to anyone at any time with regard to your fathering ever again.

Fight for 50/50 shared physical time regardless of legal cost or time.

NEVER voluntarily relinquish any of your parental rights, especially equal physical time with your children. Make sure your voice will be heard in all parenting areas and that any divorce or separation agreement clearly states this.

You may not realize the significant impact you have on your children. So many men I speak with who are divorcing believe they only deserve an every-other-weekend sharing arrangement and that the children are better served living with their mother the majority of the time. If you have these thoughts, dispel them right now. You can be as effective as anyone else in raising children. Your children deserve as much of your direct parenting time as you can give them. I believe that both parents have the right to a 50%-shared parenting arrangement and no less. Unfortunately, you may need to fight for this basic fathering right. Your children need both parents equally, and I would never suggest taking anything away from a mother. She deserves her 50% of the time as well.

You may come up against social attitudes that tell you women are better suited to raise children and that mothers should have more physical time with their children.

That is 100% wrong.

My own Foxhole Single Fatherhood proves my point. Remember, you have an equal responsibility to take care of your children and deserve equal direct parenting time with them. Fight for it even if you have to go to trial. NEVER let anyone—your ex, your lawyer, your children, a judge, a parenting consultant—tell you that you deserve less than 50% shared parenting time. The fact that you are a man is not enough evidence to prove that you are not as fit as the mother. Even if you were out supporting the family while your children's mother was home full time does not matter. Do not let anyone use these things to question your ability and right to have equal physical time with your children.

Both the mother and father deserve an equal chance to parent their children.

Even if you should lose in court, at least your children will see you fighting for them to the very end, just like a loving father should. Don't let a judge's order giving you less than 50% (equal) physical time with your children go unanswered without an appeal.

You love your children as much as their mother does, and you also want to physically raise them as much as she does. This is an extremely important message that you should send your children at all times.

Equal shared parenting time respects both parents.

Seek professional guidance immediately.

It is OK to talk to a professional, and, in fact, I recommend that all men who know they will become single fathers immediately find a counselor, therapist, or social worker they can talk to and from whom they can learn coping skills.

I personally did this, and those sessions, which I had long ago, still help me every day.

There is no bravery in suffering in silence. When you have suddenly lost your partner and home, these are some of the most emotionally and psychologically traumatic events you will ever experience. If you broke your leg, would you suffer in silence and not visit a doctor? Of course not.

I have found that we are not taught how to deal with divorce and separation, so we are not prepared. I know I was completely unprepared. It is OK to feel helpless and as if you are suspended in an emotional abyss. Those are normal feelings, and you are not alone.

So please immediately seek out a professional to discuss this new course of your life, even if you believe you feel 100% OK. It cannot hurt you.

A wonderful thing that a professional counselor/therapist can provide is understanding. It is so common to feel ashamed, emasculated, and embarrassed when your partner and home are lost. A normal reaction is to retreat from the world and get very angry. At this time of your life it is imperative to surround yourself with people who can truly understand what you are going through and who can help you realize that you are not alone and that you are not crazy. A professional counselor/therapist is perfectly suited for this phase of your life. Counseling sessions will give you a safe outlet to vent your fears, worries, and dreams, and to also shed as many tears as you need to. Be aware of the five stages of grief. You will probably go through each of these steps that are caused by the loss of such important parts of your life. They are:

1. Denial and Isolation (If you are already separated from your children's mother, you are probably beyond this one.)
2. Anger
3. Bargaining
4. Depression
5. Acceptance

Read about these. What you are going through may seem overwhelming and beyond your comprehension, but that is completely untrue. You simply need to learn how your mind and body are processing this trauma.

During counseling sessions, you can ask very important questions concerning your children, such as:

"What can I do to make this transition easier for my children?"

"What are my children going through emotionally that they may not be telling me?"

"How can I ensure that my children will grow up strong and healthy, in spite of their parents' break up?"

Of course, any good therapist or social worker's first advice will be, "Buy Foxhole Father, The Field Guide for Fathers."

I wrote this section of the book for the millions of men who may be feeling alone, frightened, rejected, helpless, and homeless. I have felt all of these things and I understand exactly how you are feeling. This section is for single fathers to have a place to go where they can be understood, appreciated, and supported through this most difficult time.

Don't feel insecure about your ability to father your children.

Many men feel insecure about child rearing. Men can be just as effective as women. Have confidence in yourself that you can handle every situation when your children are in your care. This book is meant to support you and your new life's mission. Many people believe that only women are qualified to take care of children. This is a very old-fashioned idea that has no place in the new millennium. Ignore people who share these sexist thoughts with you.

Learn to self-observe; it will help you unlearn ingrained bad habits and attitudes.

The emotional source of our reactions and choices in life are NOT cast in granite in our hearts and minds. In fact, most of what we do and think, and, most importantly, how we think, has been taught to us. Sometimes damaging relationship interactions in our past have caused us to internalize dysfunctional filters and attitudes toward life.

But like any bad and mindless habit, our learned and automatic responses can be unlearned, just like smoking.

All it takes is for you to begin to observe and analyze yourself in ways you probably never have before. If you learn how to do this, it will allow you to gain much more control in many areas of your life, not just in your relationship with your ex.

We will focus on your interaction with your ex here. It is important to understand that over time our relationship interactions can be set on a sort of autopilot. Usually we take the path of least resistance regarding many topics and for many decisions, and this becomes a silent and mostly unknown agreement between partners. Unfortunately, within these "agreements," many times there is repression of expression, and neglect of your needs being met. These types of accumulated issues may be a large part of the turmoil that has caused you to part with your ex.

At this moment, be honest with yourself and realize that your ex has been part of your emotional system for quite a long time. Removing her impact on your system will take a concerted and focused daily effort, but it can be done, and I am sure you are capable of it.

Allowing your ex to impact your emotional system is the bad habit you need break.

This book tries to help you with this as well as with so many other new and fear-inducing changes with which you and your children are faced.

I want you to have confidence in yourself. Every time you feel afraid or unsure of yourself, I want you to realize that the negative voice you are hearing is just a vestige of a bad relationship you once had with someone, possibly your ex, in which you were subjugated and emotionally mistreated.

I want you to self-observe in those fearful moments and pause. Those fearful reactions are also learned, just as your interactions with your ex are, and you don't have to have them any longer. Your self-doubt and fear are two more bad habits that may be harming you. We will break those together as well.

Just the fact that you are reading this book shows that you are a man of action and that you have the basic strength and vision to overcome any obstacles you now face.

Holidays and birthdays: Do what is best for the children.

Divorced or separated parents can get very territorial about holidays and birthdays. I have seen parents actually "split" these days in half, and the children are exchanged in the middle of the day. This is a great example of parents NOT putting the children first. It can be a terrible parenting mistake.

It is so easy for your children's holiday or birthday to get ruined when they see this competition. The children don't want or need to spend time with each parent on these days at all. Your children just want to have a peaceful holiday or birthday.

There should be very few changes to the normal child-sharing schedule during the year. In my divorce there are only four days in the entire year when we deviate from our agreed schedule. Try to do the same.

My advice:

- Choose very few days during the year to deviate from the normal schedule.
- Alternate significant days each year if necessary.
- Allow the children to stay with that parent all day.
- Agree to let the other parent stop by briefly for a hug, but never to linger.
- Birthdays should not be alternated.
- The parent who happens to have them on a birthday in the normal schedule should allow the other parent to stay and sing "Happy Birthday" and then leave.

Personal example: Christmas Day

Christmas Day can be one of the most contentious child-sharing days of the year. Why? Because many parents completely disregard their children's needs. Millions of children's holidays are ruined by the open hostility and aggression shown by their parents.

When I had to work out a sharing schedule with my children's mother, my initial thought process was completely clouded by my selfish needs. This is so common. But what did I do? I paused and self-observed and forced myself to filter these negotiations through what was best for my kids. Then it was easy.

I believe there should be very few days that deviate from the normal sharing schedule. I only have four specific days all year where my kids' schedule changes: Christmas Eve, Christmas Day, Thanksgiving, and Halloween.

In my case I have brought this to an even greater degree when it comes to putting my children's best interest first.

I not only agreed to but personally suggested that I never have my children on Christmas Day, but always on Christmas Eve. Why? Because it was best for them. I asked to always have them on Thanksgiving.

That's it. Four days all year when I have to worry about deviating from our agreed-upon sharing schedule. Birthdays aren't specifically mentioned. My children are simply with the parent whose day it is.

When I was growing up, Christmas Eve was always a significant day to my family. Since my divorce I have never had my children with me on Christmas Day. Their mother always makes Christmas morning perfect for them, and I wanted my kids to have that. I stop by their mother's and say a quick hello and exchange hugs and kisses at the door and then leave.

Please hear this next line and read it carefully.

The children don't care about the divorce or separation as much as we think.

They just want to be inconvenienced as little possible due to it. They deserve that. Especially on holidays.

They just need to know that you are there for them 24/7. Even though you don't live with your kids every day, your impact and presence can be felt much more than by fathers who do.

For holidays and birthdays, apply my first rule: "Do what is best for the children."

In the case of Christmas Day, I did that, and my kids are better for it.

I hope you found this personal letter to you, the Foxhole Single Fathers, beneficial. I became a Foxhole Single Father in 1997. I share a special kinship with all of you.

Continue on and read the chapters in this section. I wrote them to address the unique struggles that we face as Foxhole Single Fathers.

The next chapter in this section is called "Every Day Is Your Day."

Read it. Live it. It is the first chapter in this section for a reason.

Sincerely,
Christopher R. Whalen
Foxhole Father

EVERY DAY IS YOUR DAY

All days are your days.

Never tell your children that their needs are their mom's responsibility.

You need to dispel any thoughts in your mind that there are "Mommy's Days" and "Daddy's Days."

Many divorced parents make the mistake of keeping "parental score" with their ex. Especially men who are paying child support and/or spousal support can quickly come to believe that the mother of their children has more of a responsibility for the financial needs and physical needs of the children.

Even if this is technically or morally true, your children should never become aware of those feelings. It may be possible you are paying child support that includes money for your children's activities, but now they are requesting money from you for those same activities. If you feel this is their mother's responsibility, have a discussion about it with their mother directly, and never involve your child at all. Never have your children bring messages of any kind back and forth between you and their mother.

If you can afford it, pay for that activity and discuss an adjustment with their mother later.

Every day is a Foxhole Father's day, and you need to let your children know that.

The fact that your children look for you to meet their needs at any time is a blessing and a sign of fathering success.

Your mission is to take care of your children to the point where it is transparent to them. You are to become the masculine, nonjudgmental, sanctuary they can always rely on. You want them to reach out to you for any reason and at any time so they see you as an unconditional and loving provider.

The separation/divorce of children's parents is disruptive enough and can lead children to lose a sense of permanence in their lives. This is the time when you need to be a real man for them. This is the time when you need to become the provider of all things financial, physical, emotional, and psychological. This is your daily mission, and all actions need to be filtered through what is best for your children. Even though they are not with you every day, you can shelter them in a cocoon of safety, strength, and love at all times.

All too often, divorces can lead to territoriality, with the children being made to feel they are living in two places at war with each other.

Imagine how frightening and painful that could make them feel. Please do all you can to pacify these feelings in your children and these attitudes within yourself.

Children's needs can arise at any time. Your child-sharing arrangement will definitely not coincide with those needs. It doesn't matter which parent has physical control over them.

If you handle this correctly, your children will believe that every day is your day. That is a precious gift that is easy to give them.

DIVORCE DOES NOT HAVE TO BE
TRAUMATIC FOR CHILDREN

How you act during and after the divorce can make all the difference to your children.

Your children will follow your emotional lead. You can make the divorce the springboard for the rest of their lives instead of a lifelong burden. There does not need to be a stigma attached to being from a family of divorce.

My children are a perfect example of how a "broken home" can greatly enhance children's lives. How my children's mother and I handled co-parenting made their lives so much better than it would have been had we stayed married. My children have two stable and loving homes instead of one dysfunctional home. Yours can have both, too.

Children need to be nurtured, insulated, and guided firmly. There are many intact families where the parents provide none of these things. In my situation, my children were very lucky. They had two parents who always put the children's needs above their own, both when we were together and when we divorced.

I don't believe children have a universal reaction to divorce. So many things I have read over the years automatically assume there will always be some negative impact on the children, and rarely have I seen any literature discussing how beneficial it truly can be. I know it is out there, but it doesn't make the headlines. I hope this book and my experience can start to change some of the negative attitudes that still exist about divorce and children.

I have read studies that say the absence of either parent can have a negative impact on children, and the absence of a father can hurt boys more than girls. If you have sons, please keep this in mind.

I believe that children simply need their basic needs met unconditionally by both parents, regardless of the living arrangements. If the sharing arrangements consider this first, and both parents agree to a co-parenting strategy that puts the past behind them and puts the uncon-ditional care of their children first, then the children can flourish much more than they would have in a household with two parents who truly do not love each other.

You don't need to live with your child every day for them to feel insulated and loved by you. Physical closeness does not always equate to a child feeling loved and nurtured and secure.

In today's world technology allows us to be virtually anywhere we want to be. It easier now more than ever to stay connected with your children.

The children's attitudes about the divorce will flow from you. It is imperative, as I have stated over and over again in this book, that you consciously and deliberately think about everything you say and do around your children. If the parents convey that the divorce is for the best, and they continue their unconditional love, the children will see that there is no loss and no great parenting change. They will feel comfortable and pacified.

The children need to learn that life can change, sometimes dramatically for them. Over the course of their lives, there will be changes over which they have no control. You can teach them, through your example, how to navigate these changes successfully.

They have gone through a dramatic life change and will now be living in two different places. They will no longer see both parents every day.

Now is the best time to use your Foxhole Fathering skills and help them successfully deal with it. It can be done. I have proven it.

Focus on fathering them through this change, like any other. They don't have to become victims of the divorce, even though society and the media may tell them so.

Do your best to cooperate with their mother. Put aside any negative personal feelings, and hopefully she will do the same. Remember, she is also going through the same changes you are. No matter what has happened in the past, both of you played your part.

If you continue to harbor bad feelings, your children will see this, and their positive transition can be delayed.

Being the masculine presence in their lives means being the best male example you can be. A man should go forward without whining and complaining in front of his kids. A man should show only strength and a positive attitude about his family's life changes and present a positive outlook for the future.

Remember, your children should not be aware of any bad feelings you have about their mother.

Was I always successful at this? Absolutely not. I didn't have this book! I had to learn the hard way. I am very fortunate that my children and their mother were patient with me when I exposed any negative feelings.

I failed many times, but I was always self-observing and trying to be a better father for my kids every day. Even when I failed, I tried to put their needs first and knew that my needs did not matter.

All you have to do now is to follow through with your mission.

If you have had doubts that splitting up was best for the children, you can put those away. If one or both parents do not share a true romantic love, then creating separate homes as soon as possible is the best advice. The sooner the better.

Staying together for the kids is a mistake. Why? Even if there is no discord between the parents, the children are learning the wrong lessons regarding what marriage is supposed to be. The children may internalize your dysfunctional spousal relationship as normal, and possibly seek the same in the future. Scientific studies have shown that unhappy couples create unhappy kids, and the number one predictor of mental health in children is parental communication.

Some parents stay together and live in separate bedrooms! Now that you are on you way to becoming a Foxhole Father, you can see how damaging that can be.

You have taught them that should they find themselves in the same circumstances in the future, they should also do the hard but correct thing and start a new home with their children.

Have confidence that you have done the right thing by striking out on your own. Don't worry about it any longer. Take that deep emotional energy and use it to make your children's new life better than they could have imagined.

A MAN'S DEFINITION OF HIMSELF

The loss of a wife, and how much a man defines himself by her, can go beyond the grief a woman feels at the loss of her husband.

In my CPA practice, I have worked on the financial side of many divorce cases. Divorce can be emotionally devastating to both the husband and the wife.

I don't think there has been adequate attention paid to the emotional and psychological impact of divorce and separation on men.

The emotional progression that a man goes through during separation and divorce is different than what women go through. Many attitudes in society focus on supporting women and what they have been put through by men.

Many times, men are ridiculed, marginalized, and turned into villains. Quite often men, especially masculine men, are depicted as not capable of taking care of children on their own.

Men are just as emotional and sometimes much more emotional than women. Men can be more committed to the children, and men can be more devastated by divorce than women. Society needs to change the conversation from men as adversaries, unfeeling and incapable of parenting, as this is not reality. There should be a real effort to humanize men of divorce.

But men also need to be more vocal about their feelings. Men often retreat and grow silent during times of emotional stress. This can lead others to believe that they are unfeeling and cold, when the opposite is quite often true.

In my twenty-five years working daily with families going through divorce, I have seen that men's emotional experiences and their sense of loss is different from a woman's, especially when there are children involved.

Let's take an example where a couple has three children, and the wife decides that she wants to divorce the husband after ten years. The divorce is done in a collaborative and peaceful way, and the children will spend equal time with each parent.

I find that men define themselves by their relationship with their wives more than wives define themselves by relationships with their husbands, especially when children are involved.

Why is this important? Not enough attention is paid to this concept. The loss of a wife, and how much a man defines himself by her, can go beyond the loss a woman feels at the loss of her husband.

Quite often a woman defines herself overwhelmingly as a mother. The part of her that was defined by her relationship with her husband can begin to fade once children arrive. The significance of her husband to her self-definition can continue to decline over time, and the children's significance can fill that space.

But a man often continues to want and need affirmation from his wife at the same level he enjoyed it prior to children. A man's decision to form a monogamous bond with a woman stems from his desire to want to take care of her and provide for her. His success or failure at this grows into a major part of his self-definition. This appears before children are in the picture and continues after. Part of men's desire to have children stems from the feeling of wanting to fulfill a woman's dreams.

So, back to our example. It is ten years into the marriage, and the wife wants to divorce. The couple sells their marital home and buys new homes, and they start their lives as divorced co-parents.

The failure felt by a man when his wife feels that he is no longer good enough to the be the man in her life goes to the core of how he defines himself. His children also define him, and they are just as significant to him as they are to his wife. But his wife may have an easier time with the transition as the children are much more a part of her core definition than her husband is.

The husband in our example has lost a main reason for living: taking care of his wife and providing for her. He also has lost his physical home and the experience of living with his children full time. The loss of these three things can be equally devastating to men, and they happen at the same time.

The purpose of this chapter is to try to provide insight into some of the emotions you may be feeling but can't articulate. What you are going through is incredibly difficult, and no one prepares men for this.

It is OK for you to seek out professional help, especially that of a grief counselor. When a wife has left you, it is very much like a death. You can feel so many emotions, especially helplessness. I can think of no worse emotional devastation than that of a man who feels helpless and unable to fix a situation with his marriage or his family.

Be kind to yourself. One of your main self-definitions, if not the main one, has been stripped from you, sometimes in a terrible way. It can leave you feeling as if you are floating in an abyss, with no direction, no ground under your feet, and no purpose left for your life.

This is a great time to self-observe and get above your emotions. Take stock of where you are and decide on the man you want to be for your children.

Concentrate on eliminating all anger toward your ex. Being angry is not healthy for us. Anger simply means that we have given control of our emotions to something outside of us. That is a mistake. Work on defining your happiness and feelings of success by the type of man and father you are every day.

The Foxhole Single Father consciously builds a new and healthy self-definition of the man he wants to be. This starts and ends inside of him.

Once you have a clear vision of the man you want to be, then get all of the help from as many resources and people as you need to become that man.

Your ex may have done terrible and painful things to you. I would never negate your pain, but I do want to give you a different perspective. Neither of you are wrong, just wrong for each other. She is trying to find her happiness, and she deserves that. She did not have to make you happy or do things that you needed. She did the best she could. She did not have to love you forever. Don't let the actions of someone else, even the love of your life, remain a burden in your heart and mind.

Wish your ex well and co-parent with her with politeness and respect. A man can move on and not define himself by a lost love. If you can do these things with regard to your children's mother, your children will see this. Their healing from the divorce will be quick, and their creating a new definition for themselves can begin.

If you stay mired in your prior self-definition, so will your children.

DEALING WITH LONELINESS

Many of you may not have lived alone for a very long time. You were used to hearing your children's voices and the sounds of your home every day. You were used to waking up with someone and sharing your life's up and downs.

The transition to living alone part of the time was very hard for me. Up until my divorce, I had never lived alone. I had gone from living with my mother to living with my wife. I tell you this to let you know that I can truly understand many of the sad feelings you are experiencing now.

Half of my nights were now spent completely alone in an apartment, with no other family voices and sounds. It was very claustrophobic, lonely, and frightening at times. But as time went on, the sharpness of my loneliness and fear dulled. Then one day it was completely gone. This will happen for you as well. I love my divorce.

I want to stress again, as I have done in other parts of this book, to seek professional mental help to learn coping skills for this life change you are going through. There are great counselors, psychiatrists, and social workers who specialize in the exact issues you are facing every day.

I personally went to a therapist when my marriage dissolved, and I learned amazing things about myself, fatherhood, and life. With the therapist's help, I was able to fully understand how the divorce was impacting me and the kids and, more importantly, how to stop defining myself by it. I learned to create a new life path and definition for my children and me.

You may feel that no one else can truly understand how alone you are feeling. It can also be embarrassing to share the specifics of your breakup with others close to you. A therapist can be such a great part of your healing process and transition. A therapist will give you something so important. He or she will truly listen to you and understand what you are feeling. He or she will give you coping skills and help you quickly transition to your new life.

You may be going through so much right now. A mental health professional can speed your healing greatly. Allow yourself to feel all of it, process it, and heal. Attack your pain head on, and never run from it. If you do this, it will eventually run from you.

There are male support groups out there. These can be a help, but be very careful to avoid those that seem to propagate anger, especially toward women.

What you are feeling is real and normal. You are not alone, and you are not the only one feeling these things at this moment. When I first became a Foxhole Single Father, I quickly realized that men evolved to feel lonely for women. If we didn't, then our species would not exist.

A significant part of the loneliness you are feeling is genetic. When I realized this, it gave me a new perspective and understanding. Our most important human urge is to procreate. This is not conscious, but instinctive. Loneliness, along with sexual urges, is the most vital part of that.

You are battling emotions that stem from the deepest and oldest parts of your brain. You are not weak.

Romantic loneliness evolved to be brutal, especially in masculine men. If you are being crushed by it right now, then see it as confirmation that you are the most evolved creature on the planet!

I hope this gives you a new perspective on your loneliness and helps you to see that what you are going through has nothing to do with weakness. You simply need to learn as much as you can about this. Once you understand what is happening to you emotionally, you will suddenly feel your control returning. Once that happens, it becomes as easy as tearing down a wall made out of cardboard.

These ideas truly helped me to heal.

Once I had this understanding, I began the work of stopping that learned and evolved loneliness from controlling my emotional state ever again.

You can, too.

It is time to self-observe, be objective about your pain, and heal from this as soon as possible. This is for your children's sake and yours.

Don't define yourself by the loss of a partner. Never again define yourself by a woman in your life. Learn to have your satisfaction in life come from within yourself only. That is one of this book's main lessons.

Being the best possible masculine nonjudgmental sanctuary for your children should be enough to fill you with the greatest joy imaginable. Nothing else in life should give you the sense of accomplishment this gives you.

Everything else, including your personal fulfillment, is secondary.

How you handle the transition to your single life, and then how you live as a Foxhole Single Father will be great life lessons for your children.

Carry yourself with strength, love and optimism for life and for them. They will gain so much from this.

Make it your mission to move beyond your loneliness, hurt feelings and self-doubt as soon as possible, and you will.

Any doubt about your capabilities as a father were learned from bad relationships or experiences in your past, and from society's strong biases.

But there's good news. Right now you may believe your doubts and loneliness are permanently fused onto your soul, with no hope of removing them. But they are not.

I want you to listen to me and trust me. Those feelings are as thin and flimsy as Post-it notes. They can be peeled away and replaced just as easily.

You don't have to be enslaved to your loneliness, self-doubt, and sadness any longer.

The Foxhole Single Father faces his loneliness head on, sizes it up, and destroys it.

TEACHING YOUR KIDS TO RESPECT AND APPRECIATE YOU

If you want your children's respect and appreciation, always make sure you are giving the same to them.

In fact, many divorced fathers come from environments where they were not properly respected and they did not show the proper respect to their children's mother. The children may have learned disrespectful and unacceptable behaviors from both of their parents. Children may have witnessed destructive communication habits.

Many times the children will mimic these learned abusive behaviors. You have two important jobs in this case.

Job 1) Realize that your children are NOT their mother. They may say hurtful things that she once said, but try to let it flow around you without any emotional impact.

Job 2) Father them through this. They may be victims of a bad environment, which you are partly responsible for. These disrespectful behaviors are bad for your children; remember that. Your feelings do not matter. You have the strength and love to help your children unlearn all of these things.

There are times when it is OK to tell your children they should do something because you prefer it, as long as there is no harm to them in you making such a request. This book will tell you to not demonize any behavior that is essentially normal. Honoring a request from someone you love and who is dedicated to you, especially if there is no significant negative impact on you, is normal behavior.

Many single fathers have come from environments where they were not respected, appreciated, and considered. If your children show this same behavior toward you, try to undo this terrible lesson. This should be replaced with teaching them that there is a minimum level of respect that people in their lives deserve and to always show appreciation to those people.

Along with this, children should be taught to extend themselves and inconvenience themselves when they are in a close and loving relationship. Teaching the value of loving selflessness in certain situations will enhance their lives.

So, with your children it might go something like this.

It's a Friday night, and your daughter has plans to go to a late movie. This is the opening night of a film she has been waiting to see for a long time. She has been looking forward to it more than anything. You are her only possible ride home.

It is only 6 p.m., and you are so exhausted from your work week that your eyes are closing.

You should tell your daughter the truth and say that it is not possible for you to pick her up from the movies tonight. She may be disappointed, and if she expresses anger or harshness, calmly discuss the ideas in this chapter.

Tell her that it is OK for you to say no or to change plans based on your needs tonight. Ask her to take a step back and see what is really happening. Ask her to realize who you are and how you live for her every minute of every day. You are a human being first, and her father second.

Teaching this lesson of appreciation and selflessness is so important for your children's development. I am not suggesting this in any way for the father's benefit. All of this is for the children's benefit for the rest of their lives.

Teaching them that they should consider your feelings in their decisions sometimes is OK. As they mature, this becomes even more important. You will be one of the most significant relationships in their lives, and it will be the source of what they will consider normal when interacting with the broader world.

When your children show you disrespect or are inconsiderate to you, it is bad for them, not you. Try to teach them why.

TAKE CARE OF YOURSELF

The Foxhole Single Father is often very stressed and has little free time. You need to make sure you take care of yourself, because no one else will. No one else is supposed to, by the way.

Keep yourself emotionally and physically strong and happy for your children. No matter how hard you try, your children can tell how you are feeling all the time. Remember this, please. Taking care of yourself will help keep you happy, strong, and content. That is the father you want your children to see and spend time with.

One of the best ways to do this is to make sure you have down time and to do things you truly enjoy as often as you can.

It is so easy to lose our patience with children when we are burnt out. We can feel resentful and full of self-pity, and when our children are with us and need us, our reactions can hurt them.

Then we have to face the guilt that follows these types of situations.

Many of us get in a daily cycle of working, taking care of the children, going to sleep, and then starting all over again. Much of our adult lives we are serving other people, bosses, children, etc. It is almost impossible to stay happy and to feel fulfilled this way.

As an adult man, you need to have personal enjoyment that goes beyond work and children. It is not possible to be emotionally balanced, which you need to be a good father, without this.

Take time as often as possible, even a few minutes several times a day, to relax and get your mind off of work and the kids. Get up from your desk and take a walk. Spend time with friends and people who love you.

Eat lunch out of your normal workspace and clear your head.

I found that lifting weights and meditating several times each week really helped me relax.

Put taking care of yourself on your daily to-do list. Make an appointment with yourself that you always keep.

With this thought of taking care yourself in mind, I want you to know that there are times when you can't be with your children during your parenting time. This is normal and OK.

There can be work responsibilities or important personal events to attend. It is good for them to see you doing normal adult activities outside the house, especially personal ones that you highly enjoy.

Do not have guilt in these situations. Work and personal obligations can arise on any day. Do your best to minimize time away from your children when they are in your care, but realize it is a completely normal occurrence.

Your kids do not need you in their presence 24/7.

Having personal activities outside the home is a great life lesson to teach your children.

WHEN YOUR EX IS DATING

You may be living through the following right now:

Your children's mother is dating a new man who has been sleeping over in your old bed on your old sheets, while your children are sleeping in their same old rooms.

This thought can enrage and sadden you for many reasons and on many levels. No matter what, you need to get past these feelings. They can only hurt you and your children in the long run.

You also have to remember that your ex has the right to live her life in any way that she sees fit, just as you do. Accepting this fact is critical to your becoming an effective Foxhole Single Father.

Your ex has every right to do what she wants as long as the children are not in danger. Having a boyfriend sleep over usually does not put the children in any type of danger. It is important to remember that you and your ex will likely have different parenting styles.

Your children might not be in danger, but they may be uncomfortable about this stranger sleeping in their mom's bed. They may not be able to express this to her.

If you have let your children know how enraged and upset you are about this subject, the odds of your children coming to you to discuss their discomfort about it are greatly reduced.

This is a tragic mistake. Remember, what is your goal? To become the masculine, nonjudgmental, and nurturing place for them. So, you should project nothing but civil co-parenting to your children at all times, even if their mother's actions enrage you.

Back to our example. Let's say that you don't express your personal feelings about what their mother is doing. The odds are your children will come to you with their concerns and feelings about it. In your children's minds, you are open for them to talk to about it. This can be about any issue, not just our example where your children's mother has a man sharing her bed.

You want your children to feel that they can approach you at any time about anything.

You have the right to say if you disagree with their mother's choice and why you disagree. You should handle this parenting moment as any other in which your children come to you with a concern about something happening in their lives.

Many children feel extremely uncomfortable when an adult stranger is allowed to spend the night in their home, especially in the bed of one of their parents. Many adults don't realize the emotional and psychological discomfort this can instill in children of any age. Yes, these other adults who are sleeping over are not strangers to you or your ex, but they will always be strangers on some level to your children, no matter how much time they are forced to spend with them. Children may wake up scared in the night and need their parent, but the parent's room may no longer be the safe place to run to as there is a stranger there now. Imagine a child lying in bed, steeped in fear, unable to get consolation until the sun comes up.

You need to put your personal feelings aside and make sure that you are there to help your children cope with these feelings if they are having them. You must make sure that they have no barrier to discussing their mother's new living arrangements with you. If you express anger and upset feelings, the chances of your children discussing their issues with you are very low. Don't you agree?

If this happens, the children may feel that they have no safe place to discuss their fears and worries. They don't want to hurt Mom, as she seems happy, and Dad is so upset by it that they don't want to make him more upset. The children can be put in the position of considering their parents' feeling over theirs. If you have read this book, you will know that this is never acceptable.

To finish our example:

If you have handled this correctly, your children are more likely to discuss their fear and discomfort with you. This will give them the understanding, perspective, and the confidence they need to approach their mother to tell her that for them, the children, having a man stay overnight is not good for them right now.

Hopefully she will respect them and modify her behavior.

You can't control what their mother will do, and that is OK. It doesn't matter what their mother does. You just want to give your children emotional skills that will help them navigate through the situation in an open, strong, and confident way.

Tell them that in the future, they are to call you at any hour, for any reason, and that they never have to lie in bed for hours scared and alone.

You should let them know that your home is always available if they are more comfortable staying there full time for the time being.

This chapter really shows how maintaining the role of the nonjudgmental sanctuary in your children's lives is important. This is especially true when you are harboring strong negative emotions about their mother.

If you are, get help to heal from them, and never express these feelings to your children.

COMMUNICATING WITH YOUR EX

If you have healthy communication patterns with your ex that are not negatively impacting your children, you may not need to read this chapter.

But I urge you to take time to read it anyway, as there may be some insights and advice you can use, especially with regard to establishing healthy communication boundaries.

Remove all anger and malicious thoughts about your ex.

You will be forced to co-parent with your ex on a daily basis. Allowing your ex to impact your emotions deeply will only hurt your fathering. You must now calmly and deliberately begin to filter all of your actions and decisions through what is best for your children. To that end, removing all negative emotional feelings about your ex and beginning to respect her as a co-parent whose responsibilities and rights regarding the children are equal to yours will be the best thing for your children.

If you have faith that your children will always see the good and bad in both you and their mother, the fear of projecting the wrong parenting will be with you constantly. Your job is to father them through whatever life will bring them, even issues that crop up with their mother.

Do you want your children to see you as a petty, complaining, insecure, and unsure father? Of course you don't. They will follow your lead now and in the future when they have a relationship break down. You are setting up the template for how they will act if they are ever in your position.

Embodying and projecting strength, optimism, security, and independence should be your goal.

Was I always perfect? Far from it. I had many moments when I was petty, when I wallowed in self-pity and felt like a victim. My children did see some of these moments, and I wish they hadn't. But no one is perfect. I forgave myself, tried to do better the next day, and moved on.

What happened between you and your children's mother is none of their business. It gives them no benefit to hear about what led to your breakup, how you feel deeply about it, and any bad feelings you might still have about your ex. If you share these things with your children, all you are doing is piling on emotional baggage they don't need. Your children are not your friends to confide your troubles to. They should remain children.

Your children should not be exposed to communications you have with their mother, and they should never be used to deliver messages between the two of you.

Teach your children to always respect their mother, and she should do the same for you. A strong and hopeful co-parenting life in two separate homes is what you should be living and projecting.

Restrict how your ex can communicate with you.

Whether you have good or bad communication with your ex, I believe that email will suffice for 99.9% of the communication you need to have with her. You need to start setting limits and boundaries in your new home and personal space. I suggest turning off new email and text notifications on your phone when your children are with you. They deserve your undivided attention. I still turn off my cell phone when my children are with me.

Creating effective but nonintrusive means of communication with your children's mother should be something you do immediately. I suggest limiting phone conversations to only emergencies and disallow text messaging. I have my cell phone to call and text my children and my clients.

Restricting the types of communication will allow you to heal much faster and therefore start your new fathering life much sooner. Most importantly, it will allow you to focus on your children when you have them. That is the best thing that can happen for you and your children.

Restricting communication to email also allows you to be thoughtful and unemotional about your responses. It allows you to pause. It allows you to respond when you are ready to. You no longer need to immediately respond to your ex's questions or needs. Your relationship is different now, so it is OK to start acting that way.

When exchanging the children, you should have no deep conversations with their mother.

If you find that she takes the opportunity to attack you or talk about inappropriate things during the exchanges, start to wear headphones and listen to music until the exchange is done.

Prepare yourself by visualizing these scenarios. Ahead of time, in your mind, bring yourself into situations where you may be emotionally triggered. Observe the negative feelings that appear and realize that you have complete control over them. You can choose to be above those situations, orchestrating things, as opposed to being manipulated by them.

Using this tool will help you move in and out of situations without being drawn in emotionally. This is best for you and your children.

MINIVAN OR SUV?

Minivan or SUV? I had this decision to make a long time ago with small children. My "manly" side told me there was no way I would ever drive a minivan as my main vehicle, especially as a single man.

I drove every SUV I could think of. My oldest was eleven at the time, and my youngest was eight. I went to car dealerships, sometimes with my children, to look at the SUVs. The SUVs have regular car doors, and they are higher off the ground. I watched as my three daughters, especially my youngest, tried to get into the SUVs. It was almost impossible for her to get the door open, let alone move such a heavy door.

It just so happened that I looked out of the dealership window to the parking lot. A minivan had just pulled into a spot right in front of me. I had never really noticed minivans before. To me they were something moms drove.

I realized that minivans have sliding doors, and this one in the parking lot had automatic sliding doors that opened with the push of a button. I watched as kids as small as mine got out by themselves and softly pulled the handle to close the doors.

I knew I had my answer. Just a few minutes earlier, a subconscious part of me would never have allowed me to buy one, but the functionality of the minivan was what I needed for my children. It was lower to the ground and had automatic sliding doors and a fully accessible third row seat with the middle seat split in half. It was like a mini bus.

I'm so glad I had this experience and fought my male pride, especially being a single dad, and bought a minivan. These kinds of decisions are difficult for some men, but you have to be strong enough not to care about what the world thinks. At first I wasn't thinking about what was best for my children. I was putting my needs first. As soon as I put my priorities in order, the decision was clear.

That minivan was my main vehicle for many years.

What was my fathering lesson here? All Foxhole Fathers, single or otherwise, don't care what the world thinks.

I would ride down the street on a pink tricycle if my kids would benefit.

I tend to be very utilitarian with decisions. What does my family need? Why do we need it? Where can I get it? The outside world's opinion is never considered.

What were the benefits of buying this minivan instead of an SUV?

Having a minivan with accessible seating means you can drive and pick up your children because you have more seating available. I have three daughters, and each one could take a friend and we'd all fit.

I wanted to either drive or pick up, especially for activities at any great distance. I made sure I did every time.

The minivan or SUV experience became a much broader conversation within myself about how I was going to live my life.

I dropped any remaining stereotypical masculine trappings that I could find inside of me.

The next time you feel that twinge of your masculinity being questioned by a decision, take time to pause and self-observe. Ignore that twinge, and your personal needs, and use my basic Foxhole Father philosophy.

What is best for your children?

That usually makes decisions very simple.

GO LIVE WITH YOUR MOTHER!

No matter what your children do, please try to never get to the point where you tell them to go live with their mother.

It is in your children's best interest to spend as much time with you as possible. You want to make sure you constantly give them a secure and safe and open environment. I know that can be very difficult, especially with teenagers, and you can get to the point where you don't know what to do.

But please don't ever get to the point where you tell them they can't live with you any longer.

Evicting a child from his home can devastate him, even if he acts nonchalant about it, and even he has given you valid reasons to do it.

Are there ever instances where you need to remove your child from your home? Of course these things happen. There may be some kind of violence or significant drug abuse problem that needs to be addressed outside of the home. In those cases, getting your child the proper treatment outside of your home could be in his or her best interest.

If you are at the point where you are about to evict your child, you may have let your emotions get the better of you. Remember, try to never allow anything outside of you, including your children's attitudes or misbehaviors, affect your emotional system.

Always remain calm and try to never raise your voice. Your child may try to distract you from the issue at hand by raising his voice and attacking you. During those times, just pause and breathe, and bring the conversation back to the correct place. Sometimes a child's yelling and screaming is simply a smoke screen.

Always respect your children, even if they are saying harsh words to you. Even though they are using adult words, they are still children. As you have read in other parts of this book, I try to treat my teenagers as if they were newborns and realize that no matter what they're saying, I should not take it personally. Never trade personal attacks with your child.

We need to focus on the problem at hand, and what is best for our children in this situation. We need to ignore any loud and abrasive attitude and language. You can always bring yourself back to the basic Foxhole Father philosophy and ask yourself, "What is best for my child?"

The best thing is for you to remain strong and calm and respectful of your child. Your child living with you is best.

I know raising children is difficult, and many parents lose patience very quickly. They too can escalate along with their child to the point of yelling. Then there is no more productive discussion, and doors get slammed.

But the good news is if you have established the correct communication patterns beginning when your children were young, these types of outbursts will be kept to a minimum.

With my daughters these outbursts were rare, and it is because I had developed all of the strategies you are reading in this book.

Maintaining an unmoving masculine nonjudgmental sanctuary is vitally important during your child's teenaged years.

Just as small children need limits and boundaries and rules to develop properly, teenagers need them, too.

What if a child threatens to move out permanently? Don't allow this extortion to change your parenting at all. After a certain age, we cannot stop our children from living with whichever parent they choose. Just express how such a move could negatively impact them.

Especially during teenage years, children need rules and boundaries. Just know that under the surface of their complaining about those rules, they need to feel your strong presence and guidance.

In the long run they will be better for it, and they will thank you for it. My children do.

PETS

I urge all single fathers to read my Quick Action Guide section called "Pets – Daddy, We Want a Puppy!" on page 35.

HOW TO HANDLE YOUR DATING

The Foxhole Single Father verifies sexual partner health through independent third-party STD testing before physical contact is made.

STDs (sexually transmitted diseases) are much more common than you think, and much more contagious. You must take ALL precautions to protect yourself from them.

This is a national health crisis. You are at extreme risk. This is your guide to managing that risk.

All potential sex partners should be fully screened for all STDs before your sexual relationship begins. This means before the kissing stage. There can be no deviation from this. This can give you some assurance that your romantic partners are disease free. Do all you can to protect yourself from having sex with an infected person.

It takes several weeks for antibodies to appear in your bloodstream when first infected with an STD. So that means that you need to wait for a few weeks after meeting someone to get tested, which also means no physical contact. Consult with your doctor about STD incubation periods. Your partner may have been infected yesterday, but this will not appear on a test they take today!

Your male sex drive can you lead you blindly into danger. We men feel incredible desperation to get women into bed. You can be of a higher order than the apes in the jungle. Self-observe and exercise self-control.

Do you think that one-night stands are safe because you use condoms? Keep reading. Do you think that oral sex is always safe? Keep reading.

People live in a fool's paradise, believing that a condom is 100% protection against contracting STDs. Most people who have Herpes 2 (genital) do not know they have the disease, and they have NOT had any symptoms. BUT they are SHEDDING the disease, which is invisible to the naked eye and fully contagious to others. Most people do not know about "viral shedding." If you don't, start becoming an expert today. Begin here:

http://www.webmd.com/genital-herpes/news/20110412/genital-herpes-silent-spread

The first line of the article reads, "Even if they don't show any sign of infection, people carrying the genital herpes virus can infect a sex partner 10% of the time." I urge you to read the entire article until you have it memorized. Share it with every single teenage boy and man you know.

So remember, you can examine a woman in bright light and not see any physical sign that she is shedding Herpes 2. Most alarmingly, some people infected with an STD are NOT making sexual partners aware of their infections. Some people infected with Herpes 2 may be taking antiviral drugs, such as Acyclovir, to suppress the severity of outbreaks. These do NOT eliminate viral shedding and your risk of infection.

An article from the National Institutes of Health clearly states:

"Acyclovir will not cure genital herpes and may not stop the spread of genital herpes to other people." Read the rest of the article here:

http://www.nlm.nih.gov/medlineplus/druginfo/meds/a681045.html

Condom use is NOT protection enough. I have spoken to people who believe that because they have used condoms during intercourse, they were completely safe from STDs. This is not true. There is still much exposed skin where diseases can be transferred even while using a condom.

Study this article from the Centers for Disease Control:

http://www.cdc.gov/condomeffectiveness/latex.htm

The first line reads: "Consistent and correct use of male latex condoms can reduce (though not eliminate) the risk of STD transmission."

I have asked potential romantic partners if they always use condoms during oral sex. The majority do not. I direct them to scientific literature about oral Herpes 2 transmission. There is always a pause and then that moment of harsh realization that they have orally exposed themselves to STDs. Many men and women are infected with Herpes 2 in their mouths and do not know it.

Men who perform oral sex on women have oral exposure to Herpes 2 and HPV and easily contract it in their mouths. Since I have been single,

99% of women I have asked refused to get tested for STDs. I have tried to make the strong choice and walk away from them. I urge you to do the same.

Once you have Herpes 2, you will have it for life. But luckily, your safety is in your control, and you can take measures to protect yourself.

Your life hangs in the balance. The AIDS virus is still out there, so do not simply take someone's word for it that they are not infected. Most people don't know if they are infected with an STD.

If women refuse your request for testing, you must be strong enough to walk away from them. You have a responsibility to stay as healthy as possible for your children. If you fail to request that potential sexual partners be tested for STDs (some life-threatening), you are not putting your children's needs ahead of yours.

After the incubation period length, you should both consult with your doctors and get a prescription for a full STD panel. You should both agree to share the results with each other. Are you sure that your potential partner has not been intimate with anyone else since you met?

The following is your Sexual Safety Pledge.

Repeat after me:

- MY POTENTIAL SEXUAL PARTNERS AND I WILL BE TESTED for STDs before any physical contact is made.
- If a potential sexual partner refuses to be tested for STDs, I will walk away.
- I understand that this testing must happen before the kissing stage.
- We will personally review the test results together and not just take each other's word for it.

Once the STD tests are reviewed and sexual health is verified, enjoy all that dating can offer you, but always use condoms.

Be prepared for disappointments when viewing the results of your potential partners. Many people are infected but are not aware of it. I know this because many of my potential sex partners discovered they were infected with one or more STDs when I required testing.

That alone proves the validity of this chapter.

The Foxhole Single Father verifies sexual partner health through independent third-party STD testing before physical contact is made.

The next chapter, "Should I Live with Another Woman?" (page 219) continues this discussion about dating, specifically its potential impact on your children.

SHOULD I LIVE WITH ANOTHER WOMAN?

This is a fitting last chapter for the Foxhole Single Father section.

If you never live with another woman, your children will not suffer in any way. What I mean by this is that if you choose to never cohabitate while your children are growing up, this will cause them no harm. Your children will be completely comfortable living with you alone. You will have kept strangers and the rest of the world outside of the sanctuary you have created for them.

Why do I bring this up? I want you understand that you living alone with your children is the best way to ensure stability for them. If you decide to bring another woman to live with them, no matter how much in love you are with her and how fond your kids are of her, you are bringing the outside world into their home, and their sanctuary could be ruined.

Children can grow incredibly attached to a new partner you invite to live with you. Many romantic relationships simply do not last. The potential trauma and upheaval caused by the breakup of your live-in romantic partner can be devastating to children. It may reopen wounds caused when you and their mother split up.

You may get an incredible amount of pressure from people in many areas of your life to "move on" or "stop being so picky" or "make it official." This pressure can be severe, and you need to ignore it. There are many evolutionary and biological pressures that may influence you as well. They are influencing your decisions right now, without you realizing it. They can make you disregard your first and only mission: What is best for your children?

You may be given ultimatums from a woman about living together or getting married. Simply ask yourself, "Do my CHILDREN NEED me to live with her?" That is what a Foxhole Single Father does. If the answer to that question is no, then your decision is clear. Your desire to cohabitate should get much less consideration than the potential negative impact on your children.

If you ever feel that you are unable to function as a father because a woman is not living with you, realize this is not true. You have all of the tools inside of you to raise your children. It is common to go through times of self-doubt and to sometimes believe that the children need a woman as well as you in your home for it to be functional. This is also not true.

When I became single, I was overwhelmed with keeping up with cooking, housework, washing and ironing my clothes, and other domestic responsibilities. I outsourced all of those things that I could afford. You don't have to do everything yourself. There is no weakness in hiring domestic help. If you can afford it, do it for yourself.

Bringing a stranger into your children's home—yes, a woman who is not their mother is a stranger—should only be done after years of building your relationship with that person outside of your children's view. If you allow a stranger to live with your children, then you have brought the outside world into their home, and they no longer have a safe haven away from it.

It takes many years to really get to know somebody. Look at the divorce rate and the second-marriage divorce rates.

Once you have spent enough time to make sure she is right for you, then you should make an effort for your children to meet her so they can get to know this significant person in your life.

The impact on your children when spending time with your girlfriend compared to cohabitating with her is a universe of difference.

Have you ever heard of an adult in therapy at thirty years of age whose emotional issue is:

> "My father never got remarried! Why didn't he give
> me a stepmother and stepbrothers and stepsisters?"

Of course not. I don't believe it has ever happened.

That simple story should really make my point very clear and should also open your eyes to how rare your remarriage or cohabitation should be.

Because men define themselves so heavily by having a woman on their arm and in their bed, there can be a blind mission to find another one for yourself.

Especially if their mother is alive, your children have no need for another mother. There is no substitute for their biological mother. You need to fight the socialized and evolutionary urge to bring a woman into your home.

As I have discussed, you need to put all of your personal needs in the backseat and filter all of your remaining life decisions through what is best for the children.

Looking at my comment above about a stepmother and stepsiblings, you will see that the most conservative approach is to not cohabitate until your children are out of high school. This will do the most to guarantee positive development into adulthood.

This is a vital point. No matter how much you have fallen in love with a woman, the level of discomfort a child can feel (no matter how sweet and loving this woman is) is astronomical. Most children will NEVER tell you these feelings once they see how much you want to bring this female stranger into their home.

Once they start living with a non-family member, they will have to accommodate that person in their space and throughout their lives. Your dating someone is your choice, but your children living with them is completely optional.

I realize how harsh this sounds, and I have done this on purpose. When a single father is lonely, the allure of replacing this vital part of his self-definition and self-worth is intoxicating and can easily lead to blind and reckless decisions.

The Foxhole Father gives his children undivided attention in their home.

Your life is not your own. Your space is no longer your own. You are now keeping a home for your children. They are the product of a dissolved parenting partnership. They now have two separate places to call home, which can be hard enough. Your home needs to become a cocoon of safety against the perils of the world.

Your romantic life should mostly be kept away from view of your children. There is no need for the children to know about any romantic interest unless and until you feel you must marry a woman to truly better your children's lives. This is rare. And no, your increased happiness living with a woman is not justification enough.

Most romantic situations are temporary, no matter what the participants believe in the beginning. Only expose your children to substantial and permanent romantic relationships. This type of romantic relationship takes years to develop.

The negative consequences of forcing your children to live with other children they are not related to can be life altering. Stepsiblings are also strangers to your children. You have to remember that you are an adult and that you need to filter these decisions through the age and mentality of your children. Your children need to be comfortable in every way in their home. Bringing strangers into their home can make them feel constantly self-conscious and invaded by the outside world. Try to imagine how traumatic it might be to a ten-year-old girl if unrelated teenaged boys move in.

Living with another family is always unnecessary for your children. You may want it, but that does not matter. Accommodating a grown woman in their home can be hard and uncomfortable. Now imagine your children having to share their home and your time with her children. Really think hard and long before you do this to your children.

I am not saying that there will definitely be negative impacts on your children. Some blended families seem to have success. If your children's mother passed away or is absent, finding a loving stepmother can give them things that will help their development.

Children are developing through their teen years and beyond them. Maintaining a safe and comfortable environment within which a child can grow is the most important consideration here.

The parenting lesson is that even if you meet your life partner, this is only one percent of the considerations needed to decide if your children should be forced to live with her.

Your children do NOT have to accommodate ANYTHING you need if it can possibly stifle their development or reduce their comfort in their own home. I think after reading this book you will agree with me on that.

Their needs come first, and yours are secondary. The children did not have a say in the divorce. You have to be their advocate constantly, even against yourself and your needs.

So many parents say:

- "Kids are resilient."
- "I need this person in my life; my needs have to come first sometimes."
- "Showing the children a healthy spousal relationship is worth the discomfort the children will feel."
- "Millions of people get remarried every day."
- "It's my time to be happy."

None of these thoughts consider the children's best interest, so they are not worthwhile.

It is possible that bringing strangers to live with your children may be a positive experience for them, but I believe this is extremely rare.

So please take your time before changing their lives this way, and then take more time.

Your children deserve your undivided attention when they are with you.

Remember that there is almost no potential harm to your children if you never live with another woman, and exponential potential harm if you do.

ACKNOWLEDGMENTS

I'd like to thank the following people for their tireless proofreading efforts:

Mary Barlow (Mom); James Whalen (Dad); my brothers, Jim and Peter; my sisters, Mary, Sue, and Jennie; Dominick Barlow, Judith Emslie, Patricia Rahner, Eric Arauz, Kara Dillon, Ellen Batterson, Sarah McGregor, Fred Chalmers, Mitchell Mund, Frank Rubba, Don Gspann, Denise Gspann, Annette Morano, Kelly Johnston, Tom Gavornik, Joan Gavornik, Lisa Samen-Alessi, Stephanie Samen-Sullivan, George Rademacher, Diane Rademacher, Richard Bond, Patrick Donohue, Babette Deering, Ric Duncan, Mayedel Briggs, and Jennifer Corey.

To Roger Cohen and Robert Salesman, my oldest friends: An entire book could be filled with thanks to both of you.

To Nicole Braatz for graphic design work.

To Eric Arauz, who suggested I write a parenting book.

ABOUT THE AUTHOR

Christopher R. Whalen is a Certified Public Accountant and owns and manages his own accounting and consulting firm in New Jersey. He specializes in family financial matters and works with collaborative legal teams towards peaceful divorce resolutions. His volunteer work includes prisoner reentry programs and mentoring youth offenders. He lives with his children in New Jersey.

Made in the USA
Lexington, KY
12 December 2014